What they don't tell you about
MUSIC

By Nicola Barber
Illustrations by Bob Fowke

Dedicated to J.S., whose *Bach* was definitely
worse than his bite.

Hodder
Childre
Book
a division of Hodder Headline plc

Hello, I'm Wipo of Burgundy. Don't ask me why I've got such a silly name. You never know, it might catch on... Anyhow, I thought it was about time someone told you all the bits they don't normally tell you about the story of MUSIC. So here they are ...

Text copyright © Nicola Barber 1998

Illustrations copyright © Bob Fowke 1998

The right of Nicola Barber to be identified as the author of the work and the right of Bob Fowke to be identified as the illustrator has been asserted by them in accordance with the Copyright, Designs and Patents Act 1988.

Produced by Fowke & Co. for Hodder Children's Books

Cover: AND70101 Ludwig van Beethoven (1770-1827) (print) by Joseph Carl Stieler (1781-1858) Private collection/Bridgeman Art Library, London

Published by Hodder Children's Books 1998

0340 689951

10 9 8 7 6 5 4 3 2 1

Hodder Children's Books
a Division of Hodder Headline plc
338 Euston Road
London NW1 3BH

Printed and bound by Mackays of Chatham plc, Chatham Kent
A Catalogue record for this book is available from the British Library

CONTENTS

 Watch out for the *Sign of the Foot*! Whenever you see this sign in the book it means there are some more details at the *FOOT* of the page. Like here.

HOW DID IT ALL START?

It started with early humans humming a sabre-toothed-tiger-hunting tune to themselves under their breaths as they went out a-hunting...

It started with someone finding out what a lovely sound they made when they clapped their hands together...

It started when someone blew into an animal horn for a joke.

It started when someone noticed the 'twang' of their bow as a poison-tipped arrow flew through the air.

Yes, believe it or not, these were the earliest beginnings of music. After this people started experimenting with other sounds... and then they began to make simple instruments... and that's how it all got going really.

Soothing music

When civilisations started growing up, music was one of the things that people liked to do to show just how civilised they really were. Music became an important part of religious rituals, and it was used to entertain and soothe. We know quite a lot about the kinds of instruments that people played in, for example, Ancient Egypt, from relics found in tombs and from evidence such as wall-paintings. But, of course, we don't know what the music actually sounded like (because there weren't any recording studios in those days). Or do we?

Tut's toots

When the tomb of the young Ancient Egyptian king Tutankhamun was opened up in 1923, archaeologists found two silver trumpets inside. They were quite fragile, but the opportunity was too good to miss. A trumpeter inserted a modern mouthpiece into one of the trumpets and gave a quick blast. A blast from the past, in fact. Luckily the trumpet didn't shatter into small bits!

CONQUERING CORNUS

Because the Ancient Romans were conquering types, they used music to frighten the pants off people. They would march into battle with musicians blaring away on their cornus 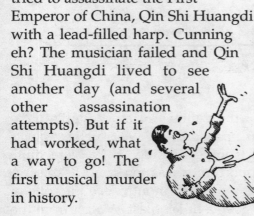 (long curly horns) making the most almighty racket until (hopefully) the opposition turned tail and fled. Someone should have told them to put a heavy metal record on - it would have had the same effect!

GLOBAL DEVELOPMENTS

Of course, music developed in different ways in different places. In India music developed in an Indian kind of way, in China it developed in a Chinese kind of way. This book tells the story of how music developed in the West (mainly Europe). Sadly, we just can't fit all those other fascinating stories in, otherwise this book would be too heavy to pick up. We can let you into one secret though. In 219 BC, a blind musician tried to assassinate the First Emperor of China, Qin Shi Huangdi with a lead-filled harp. Cunning eh? The musician failed and Qin Shi Huangdi lived to see another day (and several other assassination attempts). But if it had worked, what a way to go! The first musical murder in history.

 Strictly speaking on their *cornua* (that's an irregular Latin plural).

CLASSIC CONFUSION

Classical or not classical? What exactly is classical music? Strictly speaking Classical music is music written in the period around 1750-1827, when Haydn and Mozart were doing their stuff. But confusingly, people also use the word classical to describe all music that isn't popular - pop - music. But when Mozart was penning his greatest hits this *was* the popular music of the day. And increasingly in the 20th century the difference between 'classical' and 'popular' has become blurred, with so-called 'classical' composers borrowing all sorts of bits and pieces from 'popular' music, and so-called 'popular' musicians doing very 'classical' things too.

So 'classical' is a very mistreated word. Anyway, does it matter whether music is classical, popular or what? All the music in this book is GREAT music - otherwise it would not have been allowed in...

WIPO, NOTKER AND HERMAN

Hello again! In case you've forgotten, my name is *Wipo of Burgundy*. I'd like to introduce my friends, *Notker Balbulus* (Notker the Stammerer) and *Hermannus Contractus* (Herman the Hunchback), both fine musicians in my line of business... church music. In fact, most of this chapter is about church music and how the whole idea of writing music down got started.

NOTKER B-B-BALBULUS (840 – 912)

HERMANNUS CONTRACTUS (1013 – 1054)

The first music we know much about was the music being sung in Christian churches all over Europe from AD 500 onwards. There was probably all sorts of other music going on at the time, but we don't know what it sounded like because it was never written down. So you will just have to imagine for yourself the kinds of

Wipo of Burgundy died in 1048.

noises going on in the countryside and towns of Europe. Here are some possible ideas:

Whistling at work

Harvest celebrations with dancing

BACK TO CHURCH

Meanwhile, back in church and ignoring the cacophony of noise going on outside, monks were busy chanting. And not just monks - nuns sang church music too (see page 78). Instead of saying all the words of a service, they sang some parts to a tune called a *chant*. Actually, the tune wasn't terribly catchy or tuneful so maybe that's why it became known as *plainchant*.

For centuries, monks learned chants off by heart, then taught the chants to the next lot of monks who learned them off by heart, and then they taught them to the next lot... and so it went on. The services of the Roman Catholic Church had a particular pattern, and it was important to sing the different parts of the service in the right pattern, and to the correct chant. All the words of the services were in Latin. The centre of the Roman Catholic Church was Rome, and it was in

Rome that the pattern of services such as Mass were firmly established. There was even a special choir called the *Schola Cantorum* (Song School) which sang services in the pope's chapel. Some musicians who trained with the Schola Cantorum travelled to churches in other parts of Europe to show other musicians exactly how the chants should go...

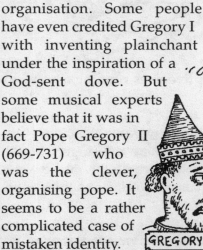

THE WRONG GREGORY?

Many people call plainchant 'Gregorian chant'. This is because plainchant and church life generally was sorted out rather thoroughly by a pope called Gregory. But which Gregory? Most books will tell you that Pope Gregory I (*c*.540-604) was responsible for this feat of organisation. Some people have even credited Gregory I with inventing plainchant under the inspiration of a God-sent dove. But some musical experts believe that it was in fact Pope Gregory II (669-731) who was the clever, organising pope. It seems to be a rather complicated case of mistaken identity.

GREGORY I

GREGORY II

A BRILLIANT IDEA

So who had the brilliant idea of writing music down?

By the 800s, there were huge numbers of long and complicated chants which had to be learned off by heart. It took years to memorise them all. One day some bright spark had the idea of writing down a few marks to help him or her remember how a tricky bit of chant was supposed to go. Or maybe lots of bright sparks had the idea all at the same time? No one knows for certain. All we know is that the earliest surviving examples of written music date from the 9th century.

Which of the following useful things do you think the first bright sparks used to write down music:

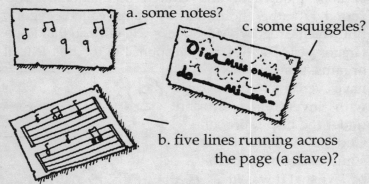

a. some notes?

c. some squiggles?

b. five lines running across the page (a stave)?

The answer is c! The squiggles were written above the relevant bit of text to show where the singer should change pitch - in other words, where the music went up, down, or stayed the same. Notes and staves were later inventions!

The first written music probably wasn't meant to be used actually in services. Instead, it was used in rehearsals as a reference by the musician, or cantor, who trained the church choir. If there was a tricky bit of chant, the cantor would look at the squiggles to remind himself how it went. Then he would teach the chant to the choir.

So much for the brilliant idea! Most 10th-century choristers were still having to learn hundreds of different chants and texts off by heart...

A MONK WITH A BAD MEMORY

Not only did Notker Balbulus (c.840-912) stammer, he also had a bad memory.

As a young monk at St Gall monastery in Switzerland, he struggled to remember the plainchants. The other monks despaired of poor Notker...

One day, a French monk came to visit St Gall. He brought with him a clever little book which showed how some verses of text fitted to various bits of chant. Notker thought this was a good idea, but he decided to improve on the lyrics.

13

He wrote his own verses and published them in a collection called *Liber hymnorum* (Book of Hymns). At the front he wrote a note describing his own youthful memorising problems:

When I was still young, and very long melodies repeatedly entrusted to memory escaped from my poor little head, I began to reason with myself how I could bind them fast...

Not only did I write great music, I was also good at astronomy, maths, clockmaking and instrument-making.

We both wrote bits of music too! Not that you will have ever heard of them...

I KNOW IT LIKE THE BACK OF MY HAND

Clearly, something had to be done before thousands of young monks had mass nervous breakdowns. Guido of Arezzo (*c*.991-*c*.1033) was a cantor at Arezzo cathedral in Italy. He claimed to be able to teach boys chants in just *two* years - previously they had taken *twelve years* for boys to learn! He devised various cunning ways of helping singers to read and remember music. For example he gave different notes different names:

ut re mi fa sol la

Many people still use these names today, except that ut is called do, and ti is added after la:do re mi fa sol la ti

Another whizzo device invented by Guido was 'Guido's Hand'. This was a diagram of a hand with different notes marked on to different fingers and joints. Singers could use it to help themselves learn bits of music. In fact, no one today knows quite how it worked, but it was obviously very useful!

ANOTHER GOOD IDEA

Up to now, alert readers will have noticed we've been talking about chant - but what, you might ask, about the accompaniment? the riffs and skiffles? the pounding bass line? Well, the answer is there wasn't any accompaniment, just one single line of melody sung in unison (together) by the choir, or solo (alone) by the cantor. Then, one day, someone (well, two people actually) tried singing a second line of melody together with the first. It sounded great! *Polyphony* was born! Guido of Arezzo liked polyphony. He called it 'soft' and 'sweet' music.

Polyphony is a clever word to describe 'sounding two or more notes together'.

15

JOLLY JONGLEURS, TITLED TROUBADOURS AND TIRED TROUVÈRES

After a long, hard day in church, some lighter forms of entertainment were a welcome change. This was provided by men and women called *jongleurs* or *minstrels* depending on where they were. They travelled from village to village, or court to court. They could do almost anything in the entertainment line!

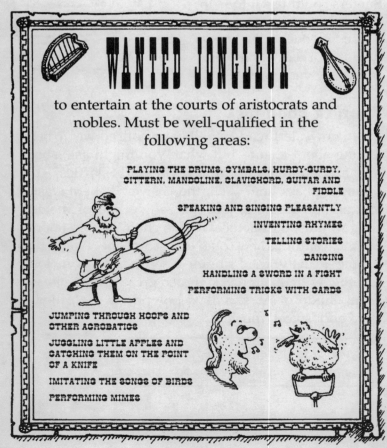

WANTED JONGLEUR

to entertain at the courts of aristocrats and nobles. Must be well-qualified in the following areas:

PLAYING THE DRUMS, CYMBALS, HURDY-GURDY, CITTERN, MANDOLINE, CLAVICHORD, GUITAR AND FIDDLE

SPEAKING AND SINGING PLEASANTLY

INVENTING RHYMES

TELLING STORIES

DANCING

HANDLING A SWORD IN A FIGHT

PERFORMING TRICKS WITH CARDS

JUMPING THROUGH HOOPS AND OTHER ACROBATICS

JUGGLING LITTLE APPLES AND CATCHING THEM ON THE POINT OF A KNIFE

IMITATING THE SONGS OF BIRDS

PERFORMING MIMES

Then the aristocrats decided to get in on the act. They began to write poetry and set their poems to music. These noble musicians were known as *troubadours* and *trouvères*. The troubadours came originally from southern France; the trouvères from northern France. Of course, juggling little apples and performing tricks with cards was rather below their dignity - they tended to write poems about more lofty subjects such as love.

The first troubadour we know of was William IX, Count of Poitiers and Duke of Aquitaine. In fact, many later troubadours and trouvères weren't nobles at all but people of humble birth who gained entry into court life because of their musical talents. One troubadour was the son of a servant, another was an orphan abandoned 'at the door of a rich man'. One of the most famous of the trouvères, Adam de la Halle (*c*.1237-87), was the son of a middle-ranking official in Arras.

Being a travelling jongleur, troubadour or trouvère was hard work. There were no trains or cars to whisk people from one place to another. The more successful troubadours and trouvères could afford a horse. But for many musicians the only means of travel were... two weary feet.

A Mass of Composers

The songs of the troubadours and trouvères were usually one-line melodies with accompaniment provided by whatever instrument the musician could turn his or her hand to - the harp, or the fiddle perhaps. But in the churches, musicians were experimenting with polyphony 👣 . Two voices singing together made some great sounds. Why not three voices... or even four? By around the 13th century, the possibilities of polyphony were making musicians all over Europe jump up and down with excitement. Composers began to write polyphonic love songs, polyphonic dance music, polyphonic hunting songs... They wrote pieces in which the different voice parts sang different words all at the same time. They used bits of plainchant as a starting point and wove the other voices around the chant. The possibilities were endless! Polyphony had arrived!

The way music was written down also became more precise. Different shapes were used to show how long a note should be. The notes were put on to lines, called a stave, to show what pitch the notes should be. Things had moved on since the time of squiggles 👣!

~ non dui ~

 To remind yourself about polyphony and squiggles look back to pages 15 and 12.

An idea for St Valentine's day

Love songs continued to be a major industry. One composer, Baude Cordier, decided to write a love song as a New Year present for his girlfriend. He called it *Belle, bonne* (Beautiful, good lady). It was written down in the shape of a heart. Another set of love songs was published in a heart-shaped book. You could try this for next St Valentine's day!

The first famous composer?

Machaut was a respected and famous composer in his own day, and is still well-known. This is mainly because he wrote down and collected together his musical works into books which still survive today. So we know a lot about him and about his music.

Curriculum Vitae
Name: Guillaume de Machaut
*Born: c.*1300 in Rheims, France
Died: 1377
Occupation: canon at Rheims Cathedral;
musician; composer; poet; civil servant in the
court of King of Bohemia and later at French court
Hobbies: falconry; horse-riding
Illnesses: bad gout and blindness in one eye, but survived the Black Death which swept across Europe in the late 1340s
Main claim to fame: wrote the earliest surviving polyphonic setting of the Mass , for four voices. Although Machaut is most often remembered for his setting of the Mass, he wrote all sorts of other music too.

 The Mass is the most important ritual of the Christian Church. In the Roman Catholic Mass, some parts are spoken and some are sung.

Rebirth experiences

The time from about 1450-1600 is known as the Renaissance. Artists, writers and other brainy types of the time decided that they didn't much like what had been happening for the past few centuries. They preferred instead to look back to the ideas of the Ancient Greeks and Romans. As Erasmus (one of the brainy types) said: 'The world is coming to its senses as if awaking out of a deep sleep.' Renaissance means 'rebirth', which describes what they thought was happening.

In fact, the ideas of the Renaissance were probably more important for art and literature than for music. Composers kept on experimenting with polyphony, sometimes with some startling results (see Thomas Tallis page 22)! However, one development that did have a big effect on music was the invention of printing:

1. Before the 1470s, all music was copied out by hand. This was a long and time-consuming process.

2. Towards the middle of the 15th century, Johann Gutenberg developed a printing press in the city of Mainz, Germany.

3. By the end of the century, the first music books were being printed and the music printing business began to flourish.

4. People bought books of music to sing or play at home.

GETTING PAID

Unless they happened to have money themselves, most composers in the Renaissance and after needed to have a wealthy patron to support them. Some composers worked for the Church, some worked for a rich aristocrat or noble. Sometimes relations got a bit strained, especially when actually *paying* for a piece of music just seemed to slip a patron's mind...

TOP TIPS FROM TOP RENAISSANCE COMPOSERS

Here are some top Renaissance composers with a selection of their Top Tips for dealing with difficult patrons!

JOSQUIN DES PREZ

Born: c.1440
Died: 1521
Patrons: Cardinal Ascanio Sforza in Milan, Louis XII of France, Este family in Ferrara

Life and music: A very successful musician and composer who wrote about 18 Mass settings and hundreds of songs and other pieces. Like other composers of the day, he sometimes used a popular folk song as the basic tune for a Mass setting.

Top tip: Josquin was quite keen on money, probably because he didn't have much. He once dropped a subtle hint to one of his patrons by writing a piece called: *Remember thy word unto thy servant*. When the patron took the hint and paid up, Josquin wrote another piece: *Lord, thou hast dealt graciously with thy servant.*

THOMAS TALLIS

Born: c.1505
Died: 1585
Patrons: English monarchs in succession - Henry VIII, Edward VI, Mary Tudor, Elizabeth I

Life and music: Elizabeth's father, King Henry VIII, had broken away from the Roman Catholic Church due to a disagreement over wives. (The

Pope refused to allow him to divorce a wife he'd got tired of.) Henry set up a new church in England, known as the Anglican Church. Tallis wrote music for the new Anglican Church. He worked at the Chapel Royal as a composer and organist.

Top tip: Tallis produced one of the most extraordinary pieces of choral music when he wrote *Spem in Alium* for no less than forty singers (eight five-part choirs). Tallis may have written this piece for Queen Elizabeth's fortieth birthday.

GIOVANNI PIERLUIGI DA PALESTRINA

Born: c.1525
Died: 1594
A.k.a.: *Palestrina* is the name of the town, near Rome, where the composer was born.
Patrons: various popes in Rome
Life and music: wrote huge amounts of successful church music including over 100 Mass settings.
Top tip: Around the 1550s, some people in the Catholic Church became very worried that church music was getting too frivolous (what about all those masses based on popular songs for a start?). They wanted to go back to good old, straightforward Gregorian chant. However, the story goes that Palestrina wrote a six-part Mass setting of such perfection that he single-handedly saved the whole future of polyphonic music. (It probably didn't happen *quite* like this!)

WILLIAM BYRD

Born: 1543
Died: 1623
Patron: Queen Elizabeth I of England
Life and music: Catholics had a dangerous
time in England after Henry VIII's tiff with the
Pope (see Tallis). Yet Byrd managed to remain a
Roman Catholic and hold the post of organist in
Elizabeth's Chapel Royal. He wrote music for
both Roman Catholic and Anglican services.
Top tip: Byrd shared the post of organist at the
Chapel Royal with Thomas Tallis. In 1575, Queen
Elizabeth gave Byrd and Tallis the right to
publish all printed music in England. So if you
wanted to print a piece of music, you had to be
nice to them! What's more, if you needed some
manuscript paper to write your piece down,
guess who you had to ask?!

GIOVANNI GABRIELI

*Born: c.*1555
Died: 1612
Patron: the government of
Venice, called the Council of Ten
Life and music: Giovanni took over as choirmaster
at St Mark's Cathedral from his uncle, Andrea
Gabrieli. St Mark's was so huge that it had two
organs, and Giovanni often divided his choir into
separate groups which sang from different parts
of the building. This technique was called *cori
spezzati* or 'spaced choirs'.
Top tip: Keep it in the family - Giovanni was on to
a good thing when he got the St Mark's job.

24

CARLO GESUALDO

Born: c.1561
Died: 1613
Titles: Prince of Venosa, Count of Conza, Lord of Gesualdo, Marquis of Laino, etc. etc.
Patron: no need of one due to noble birth
Life and music: Was passionate about music from an early age. Also passionately jealous when he discovered that his (first) wife had taken a lover. On discovering the two together, he murdered them both. It was also rumoured that he murdered his son. Gesualdo was found guilty, but because he had so many titles he was let off pretty lightly. He even married again (brave woman!) - and some people claim that he got his come-uppance when his second wife was responsible for his death in 1613.
Top tip: Being an infamous murderer didn't seem to do Gesualdo's musical career any harm, as he successfully published several sets of madrigals It's probably not advisable to go to such lengths, however.

 Madrigals are songs set for several voices. They are usually about love.

A DRAMATIC TURN

And now we come to a momentous and dramatic occasion in the story of Western music: the invention of OPERA! Operas are renowned for their ridiculous plots (more about those later), the length of time it takes the hero to die, and fat, wobbly ladies singing loud, wobbly notes...

But was it always like this?

LYRIC PROBLEMS

Date: the 1590s
Place: Florence, Italy

It all started in meetings of a kind of composers' club called the *Camerata*. In typical Renaissance fashion, the composers in this club looked back to the Ancient Greeks for their inspiration. They wanted to recreate the kind of spectacle and music seen and heard in Ancient Greek theatres. They had absolutely no idea what Ancient Greek music actually sounded like, but that didn't put them off.

They decided that what was wrong with polyphonic music was that you couldn't hear the lyrics. There were so many lines of music all weaving around each other in perfect polyphony that the words completely disappeared in a haze of harmony. The singers could have been singing 'Rhubarb, rhubarb' and no one would have known!

The *Camerata* composers decided to make the words the most important thing in their music. They wrote music with a solo vocal line that followed the stresses and rhythms of the words themselves, rather than making the words fit into a particular tune. Rather like this:

> Hello! Mynameis OrFEo. Iama CHARacter from oneofthe EARliest OPeras. I gotothe UNDERworld to REScue my wife, EUriDIce. Turnto page 28 to FINDout what HAPpens!

The vocal line was given a very simple instrumental accompaniment, so that the words came across loud and clear. This new style of music was known as *monody* (not to be confused with monotony).

THE VERY FIRST OPERA?

There is some confusion about what, in fact, was the very first opera. One of the *Camerata* composers, Jacopo Peri (1561-1633), wrote an opera called *Dafne* which was performed in the Florence carnival of 1597, but most of the music has been lost so we don't know much about it. Then in 1600, opera made its big breakthrough at the wedding of the French king Henry IV and a rich Florentine heiress called Maria de' Medici. While Peri and another *Camerata* composer, Giulio Caccini (1545-1618), squabbled and bickered over who should write the music for an opera called *Euridice*, the most important entertainment for the wedding was an all-singing, all-dancing production full of special effects called *Il rapimento di Cefalo*. The audience loved the gigantic monster that emerged from the sea, the glittering, gold chariot drawn by four (real) horses and the cloud machines that constantly changed their shape. Who cared about the music?

THE FIRST REAL OPERA COMPOSER

One of the guests at the wedding of Henry IV and Maria de' Medici was the Duke of Mantua. Not to be outdone, he decided that he would put on operas at his court in Mantua. And he knew just the man to write them, his director of music - Claudio Monteverdi (1567-1643).

You can forget Peri and Caccini - Monteverdi was the first *real* opera composer, and his operas are still performed today. However, the choice of story for his earliest opera wasn't exactly original. Monteverdi chose the Ancient Greek myth of Orpheus and Euridice but instead of calling his opera *Euridice* like Peri and Caccini, he called it... (you've guessed it) *Orfeo*.

SPOT THE DIFFERENCE

The Ancient Greek myth tells the story of Orpheus and Euridice like this:

Orpheus is a poet and singer who charms people and animals alike with the astounding beauty of his music.

28

Tragedy strikes when Orpheus's wife, Euridice, dies. She goes off to the home of the dead - the Underworld.

Orpheus is grief-stricken. He decides to go into the Underworld to win Euridice back.

Orpheus uses the power of music to persuade the gods to release Euridice. But there is a catch: on the way out of the Underworld Orpheus must not look round to see if Euridice is following...

And of course, he does. Euridice is taken back to the land of the dead and the story ends in grief and tragedy.

Or does it?

Peri and Caccini may have disagreed about most things, but they were both absolutely certain that grief and tragedy were not suitable for a wedding celebration. So they changed the ending: Euridice escapes the Underworld and the couple live happily ever after. Monteverdi remained truer to the original myth. His Euridice is sent back to rot in the Underworld. Orpheus, meanwhile, is taken off in a cloud machine by the god Apollo to live in the heavens (happily ever after, presumably).

DIFFICULTIES IN THE LIFE OF... MONTEVERDI

Being a composer in the 17th century was no bed of roses. Monteverdi had the usual difficulties with getting paid: the Duke of Mantua employed a rather tight-fisted accountant who seemed unwilling to spend any money on fripperies such as music... After months without any money at all, Monteverdi was eventually forced to write direct to the Duke: 'This humble petition of mine comes to you with no other aim but to beg Your Highness kindly to direct that I receive wages amounting to a total of five months...'

Then there was the danger of boring your patron. The Duchess of Mantua thought that Monteverdi's second opera *Arianna* was very boring and told him so. He had to stay up for nights on end trying to think of things to make it more exciting.

Finally, poor old Monteverdi couldn't even rely on his artistes. Only a few days before the first performance of *Arianna* his leading lady died of the smallpox. Very inconsiderate! Monteverdi was quite upset as she was a good friend of the family. He also had to teach the part to another soprano. More sleepless nights...

OPERA GOES PUBLIC

Opera spread quickly around the courts of Italy and other European courts. It was the latest craze! Every self-respecting nobleman wanted a little opera of his own! In Venice, the first public opera house opened in 1637. Now, opera wasn't just an entertainment for nobles and their courtiers. Ordinary people could pay to go and watch it too. Opera was a huge success.

The people who ran the public opera houses wanted to make money, so they weren't interested in operas with huge casts and choruses (too much money spent on singers). The operas written for the Venice opera houses tended to have small casts with only a few singers, no chorus, and a small orchestra. One thing that the opera houses could not skimp on, however, were the special effects. An opera without special effects would have been like *Jurassic Park* without the dinosaurs!

Monteverdi wrote two operas for the public opera houses in Venice. *The Return of Ulysses* had enough special effects to keep even a Venetian audience amazed:

BACK TO COURT: THE LIFE AND TIMES OF LULLY

The first opera composer to achieve real international fame and fortune was Jean-Baptiste Lully (1632-87). He liked to claim that he came from a noble family, but he was in fact the son of an Italian miller. Lully was born near Florence, but he was taken to France as a child. He became known as a witty fellow, a good violinist and an excellent dancer. As luck would have it, King Louis XIV was a keen dancer too and Lully soon found a place for himself at the French court.

Lully was a talented musician, but he was also a smooth operator! Like everybody else at the French court he flattered the King outrageously. The King responded by putting Lully in charge of music at court. Lully had great fun writing hugely extravagant operas that included quite a lot of dance, to keep the King happy.

LOUIS XIV KNOWN AS THE 'SUN KING'

King Louis XIV employed a ridiculous number of musicians to provide him with music wherever he went, and at whatever time of day or night. There were the thirty-six musicians to play when the king went hunting, or out for a picnic, or when there was any kind of outdoor procession or celebration. Then there were the fifty or so chamber musicians who played for dinners, ballets, balls and any other indoor occasions when the king just had to have music.

Lully organised all these musicians for the King, and he made a good job of it too. His orchestra was renowned for its fine playing. This might have been because the players were terrified - play a note wrong and Lully was likely to smash your violin over your head!

FREDERICK THE GREAT IN CONTROL

The tradition of opera as a court and a public entertainment continued to develop across Europe. One of the keenest of all kings was Frederick the Great of Prussia. He just couldn't get enough music! He loved performing on his flute, he even wrote his own music, and he often moved his courtiers to tears with the beauty of his playing... But his pride and glory was his opera house.

The King left nothing to chance: his new opera house was to be the biggest, best and most expensive in the whole of Europe! He oversaw the designs, and kept strict control over the building work. Even he couldn't work miracles, though. On the first night in 1742, the glittering audience had to clamber over workmen's rubble to get to their seats.

Frederick employed several well-known composers to run music at his court. But he couldn't bear not being in control! He trained the singers, he wrote the words for some of the operas performed at his opera house, and if he didn't like the music - he changed it. What's more, if a rebellious singer or dancer caused trouble they were quite likely to find themselves languishing in one of Frederick the Great's not-so-comfortable prisons!

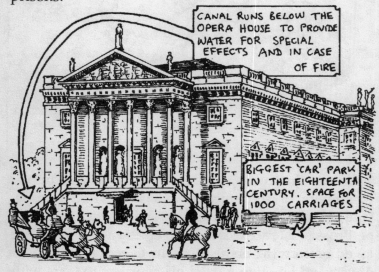

CANAL RUNS BELOW THE OPERA HOUSE TO PROVIDE WATER FOR SPECIAL EFFECTS AND IN CASE OF FIRE

BIGGEST 'CAR' PARK IN THE EIGHTEENTH CENTURY. SPACE FOR 1000 CARRIAGES

Just over 100 years after its completion, Frederick the Great's masterpiece burned down.

OPERA TERMS

Sound knowledgeable about opera by using a few of these essential opera terms:

aria basically a solo song with orchestral accompaniment in an opera (or oratorio or Passion - see page 41)

chorus the chorus is a group of people who sing together. A chorus usually has four main voice parts - sopranos (high females) mezzos (lower females) tenors (high males) and basses (low males). The chorus sing choruses which contrast with arias in an opera.

da capo aria people will be very impressed if this rolls off your tongue! A da capo aria goes like this. Singer sings tune *A*. Then she/he sings an elaboration of tune *A* which we shall call *B*. Then (deep breath), she/he goes right back to the beginning and sings tune *A* again.

recitative a sort of cross between speaking and singing. The singer sings words to notes, but the rhythm of the notes is free according to the stresses of the words. Recitative is used in operas to tell bits of the story and move the plot on. At the end of a recitative there is often an aria which slows the plot down.

HANDEL, BACH AND THE BOYS

This chapter is mainly about Johann Sebastian Bach (1685-1750) organist, composer and genius and NOT to be confused with:

> *Johann Ambrosius Bach* (father) musician
> *Johann Christoph Bach* (uncle) musician
> *Johann Christoph Bach* (first cousin) musician
> *Johann Christoph Bach* (brother) musician
> *Wilhelm Friedemann Bach* (eldest son) musician
> *Carl Philipp Emanuel Bach* (2nd son) musician
> *etc...* (there were a lot of musicians in the Bach family)

JS BACH

CURRICULUM VITAE

Born: 21 March, 1685, Eisenach, Germany

Died: 28 July, 1750, Leipzig, Germany

Married: Maria Barbara (his second cousin, the Bachs liked to keep things in the family!) who died in 1720; Anna Magdalena (also from a family of musicians)

Children: seven children by Maria Barbara; 13 children by Anna Magdalena. No less than ten of Bach's 20 children died before they reached their fifth birthdays. Five were called Johann, there was one Johanna, two Reginas, two Christianas, one Christine, two Christophs and two Christians.

Jobs: Organist in Arnstadt, Mühlhausen, Weimar, court

musician in Cöthen, director of music at St Thomas's School, Leipzig

No. of days in prison: 27. Bach's employers in Weimar were very unwilling to let him go off to Cöthen. So unwilling, in fact, that they locked him up. Bach made good use of the time by composing some organ music. In the end, Bach won. He went to Cöthen leaving the Weimar crowd looking a little foolish...

Life's work: not only did Bach produce a lot of children, he also wrote a lot of music including:
more than 200 cantatas ●◄
lots of organ music
7 motets ●◄
2 Passions ●◄
5 Mass settings
lots of keyboard music
concertos ●◄ and other orchestral music
JS Bach did not write any operas!

SIX EPISODES IN THE LIFE OF *JS BACH*

1. Bach's first job was as organist in the New Church in the city of Arnstadt. It was a cushy job! Bach had to play for a few services every week, and train the choir. Unfortunately the choir wasn't very good. Bach had little patience with untalented musicians (there weren't any in his family) and ended up fighting in the street with one of his choristers. Bach seems to have been the better fighter, but his employers weren't very amused!

You can find out on page 39 onwards what exactly cantatas, motets, Passions and concertos are.

2. To escape from Arnstadt, Bach asked if he might go to Lübeck to visit the famous organist, Buxtehude. His employers were probably glad to see the back of him for a while, so they said he could go for four weeks. Bach stayed for four months. Buxtehude was so impressed with Bach  that he offered him his job. However, there was one drawback. Bach would also be expected to marry Buxtehude's daughter. Bach said no thanks and returned to the loving embraces of Maria Barbara in Arnstadt.

3. Bach was a brilliant organist. One listener described his playing like this: 'His feet flew over the pedals as though they had wings, and powerful sounds roared like thunder through the church.' Bach himself was fairly blasé about his talents: 'There is nothing to it. You only have to hit the right notes at the right time and the instrument plays itself.' Easy, peasy!

4. In May 1720, Bach went away to Carlsbad leaving behind his wife and their four children in perfect health. By the time he returned in July, his wife was dead and buried. There was no way of sending a message quickly over such a long distance, so Bach knew nothing of the bad news until he walked through his own front door...

5. Bach quickly remarried, to Anna Magdalena, and in 1723 moved to Leipzig. At St Thomas's School he was expected to teach music, grammar and Latin. He wasn't too keen on the grammar and Latin bits. After 1734, he also had a problem with the headmaster who thought that music was rather a waste of time. Despite all this (and producing 13 more children), Bach found the time to write some of his most brilliant music including the *St John* and the *St Matthew* Passions.

6. At the end of his life Bach had eye trouble (all those years writing music by the light of a flickering candle). An English doctor who claimed to be able to treat blindness performed two operations on Bach's eyes. They didn't work and Bach died a few months later. Anna Magdalena, widow of one of the greatest composers that ever lived, spent the rest of her life in poverty.

EVERYTHING EXCEPT OPERA

JS Bach wrote virtually every kind of music except for opera. Here is your easy-reference guide to some of those words that appear on the back of CDs of JSB's greatest hits:

cantata before Bach's time, publishers used the Italian word 'cantade' on the cover of a book of music to show that this was a piece for singing. By Bach's time a cantata was a piece with either solo or choral singing (or a mixture of both). The singers were usually accompanied by a small orchestra. JSB wrote hundreds of cantatas, mostly to be performed during the Sunday service at St Thomas's Church in Leipzig. He wrote some fun cantatas too, including one in which the heroine has become addicted to the latest craze in Germany - coffee (it's called the *Coffee Cantata* in case you were wondering!).

concerto in a concerto the sound of a solo instrument is contrasted with the sound of an accompanying group of instruments. In fact, in JSB's day there were two kinds of concerto: the solo concerto with one solo instrument, and the concerto grosso with a group of instruments (often three) playing a solo part. Today, JSB's best-known concertos are probably the ones he wrote for the Margrave of Brandenburg (called the *Brandenburg Concertos*). The Margrave asked Bach to write some music for him after hearing him play. Bach sent the six concertos in a nice, neat copy but it seems that the Margrave never even opened the music. He certainly never sent Bach any payment for all his hard work...

motet a motet is a piece for unaccompanied choir. Motets were big in Renaissance times when Josquin, Palestrina and the rest were busy writing all that polyphony. JSB continued the tradition, though, and wrote several with German words for funerals, and one for a birthday.

Oratorio JSB may not have written any operas, but he did write oratorios. An oratorio is like an opera except without any costumes or acting or scenery (that leaves just the music). Oratorios were usually about religious subjects. JSB wrote one about Christmas and one about Easter.

Passion a Passion is the name for an oratorio based on the subject of Jesus Christ's trial and crucifixion. JSB probably wrote five, but only two have survived to this day, the *St Matthew Passion* and the *St John Passion*. The Passions have some great crowd scenes (sung by the chorus) and the story is told by a character called the Evangelist, sung by a tenor soloist.

GEORGE FRIDERIC HANDEL

JS Bach and George Frideric Handel were born in the same year about 120 kilometres apart, yet throughout their long lives they never met each other. It wasn't for lack of trying! They kept nearly bumping into each other all over the place. Like Bach, Handel went to Lübeck to visit Buxtehude, and like Bach he was put off the job by the daughter problem (see page 38)! Unlike Bach, Handel loved foreign travel and he *adored* composing operas. His first opera was performed before he reached the age of twenty.

In 1710, Handel got a job as director of music at the court of the Elector of Hanover, in Germany. However, the idea of spending time in Hanover didn't seem to appeal at all and he headed off to London as soon as possible. Over the next few years he spent more time in London than doing his job in Hanover. Then, in 1714, the British queen died, and the Elector (prince) of

Hanover became the new king, George I. Was Handel flung into the Tower of London by the new king? Not a bit of it. George I was rather pleased that his director of music was such a big hit in town. Handel composed the *Water Music* for a celebration water party and everyone carried on as normal.

Handel spent the rest of his life in London. He continued to compose operas but insisted on writing them in Italian. When the British public got tired of operas in Italian (they really preferred them in English), Handel turned to oratorios instead. He had more luck with these - particularly with his most famous work of all, *Messiah*. The first performance of *Messiah* was in Dublin on 13th April 1742. So many people wanted to hear the new masterpiece that ladies were asked to leave off the hoops inside their skirts.

When Handel died in 1759 he was a well-loved figure in London and over 3000 people went to his funeral in Westminster Abbey.

Handel's music caused one of the biggest traffic jams of all time. When the *Fireworks Music* was rehearsed in a park in London in 1749, over 12,000 people went along to listen. The roads were blocked for miles around. At the actual performance there was a bad fire and hundreds of people were injured.

CLASSIC TIMES

FRANZ JOSEPH HAYDN 👍
LIFETIME HIGHLIGHTS
AND LOWLIGHTS 👎

👍 1732: born 31 March, Rohrau, Austria. Just misses being an April Fool.

👎 1740: becomes choirboy at St Stephen's Cathedral, Vienna. Good musical education but not much food to eat! Haydn later called this the 'time of starvation'.

👎 1749: expelled from school after cutting off a fellow pupil's pigtail! No money, nowhere to go. Luckily he bumps into a friend who gives him food and lodging. Haydn starts to give music lessons to make some money.

👍 1759: after ten years of making musical contacts in Vienna, gets first proper job as director of music to Count Ferdinand Maximilian von Morzin.

👎 1760: gets married - but to the wrong sister. Haydn fell in love with one of his pupils, Josepha Keller. Unfortunately she decided to go into a convent rather than marry him. So Haydn married her (much less pretty) sister, Maria Anna, instead. Disaster! Maria Anna had no interest in music and is reputed to have used Haydn's musical manuscripts to line her cake tins and curl her hair...

👍 1761: becomes assistant director of music to Prince Paul Anton Esterhazy at Eisenstadt,

Austria. Start of over forty years in the employment of the Esterhazy family. Composes lots of symphonies.

👍 1766: becomes director of music to Prince Nikolaus Esterhazy. The Esterhazy household moves to Prince Nikolaus's new palace built on a swamp near Vienna. The new palace is called Esterhaza, and it has its very own opera house and puppet theatre. Haydn composes lots of operas.

👎 1790: Haydn writes 'It is really sad always to be a slave... I am a poor creature!' Not surprisingly, after almost thirty years he is rather tired of the Esterhazys and Esterhaza.

👍 1791: Escape! After the death of Prince Nikolaus, Haydn sets out for London - his first great adventure! A big hit wherever he goes. This was probably the first time Haydn had conducted a performance of his music for an enthusiastic public crowd rather than a refined court audience.

👍 1791: hears Handel's *Messiah* performed with over a thousand singers and players. Inspires him to write the oratorio *The Creation* (1798).

👎 1792: takes on Beethoven as a pupil. Finds him talented but disrespectful.

👍 1808: despite ill health Haydn manages to attend a performance of *The Creation* given in his honour in Vienna. Even Beethoven goes to pay tribute to the master.

👎 1809: Haydn dies a not-very-peaceful death - Napoleon's troops are bombarding Vienna and cannon balls are flying thick and fast through the air.

How to be a court composer

Haydn spent a large part of his life working for the Esterhazys. His job description looked something like this:

1. Joseph Haydn shall appear before the Prince neatly dressed in white stockings, white linen, with hair powdered and in a pigtail.

2. Joseph Haydn shall treat the musicians under his authority with kindness and modesty, and shall behave himself in such a way as to set a good example.

3. Joseph Haydn shall appear every day at around midday to enquire whether a musical performance is commanded.

4. Joseph Haydn shall deal with petty quarrels and squabbles among the musicians.

5. Joseph Haydn shall take charge of the music and musical instruments and make sure they are kept in good order.

6. Joseph Haydn shall train the female singers who visit the court.

7. Joseph Haydn shall compose such pieces of music as his Serene Princely Highness may command.

In return, Haydn received food, board, and a supply of uniform. He also had some freedom to experiment with the music he was composing as long as his Serene Princely Highness didn't disapprove. The down side to this arrangement was that much of the music composed by Haydn, especially his operas, was performed to an audience of the Serene Princely One (possibly plus a few servants). He also had to write a lot of pieces for the baryton, an instrument which no one has ever heard of since, but which the Serene Princely Highness Nikolaus loved to play.

HAYDN'S FAREWELL

or *How to drop a subtle hint*

Prince Nikolaus loved his vast new palace at Esterhaza and was quite happy to stay there all year round. Others weren't so keen. Although the Prince himself had several hundred rooms to choose from, he had somehow overlooked the need to build living quarters big enough for his orchestral players *and* their families to live in. The players only saw their wives and children during the holidays. One year, the Prince just seemed to forget about holidays. The players asked Haydn to *do something*! So Haydn wrote a new symphony with an unusual last movement. When it was performed in front of the Prince, each player in turn finished his part, packed up his instrument, blew out his candle and left, leaving just two violins to finish the music. The Prince got the hint, the players got their holiday and the symphony got the nickname the *Farewell*.

HAYDN AND MOZART

This is what Haydn said to Mozart's father after listening to Mozart perform in 1785: 'I tell you before

God as an honest man that your son is the greatest composer known to me either in person or by reputation...' In fact Mozart admired Haydn just as much as Haydn admired Mozart. Mozart wrote six string quartets for Haydn. Haydn attended the rehearsals of Mozart's opera *Cosi fan Tutte* in Vienna and it is said refused to write any more operas himself because he was so overwhelmed by Mozart's genius. When Haydn travelled to London he tried to persuade Mozart to go with him. If Mozart had accepted, the story of music might have been very different...

JOANNES CHRYSOSTOMUS WOLFGANGUS THEOPHILUS-GOTTLIEB-AMADEUS MOZART
CURRICULUM VITAE

Born: 27 January, 1756, Salzburg, Austria
Died: 5 December, 1791, Vienna, Austria.

Family: Parents, Anna Maria and Leopold Mozart. Leopold was a court musician and composer in Salzburg. As soon as he realised how talented his son was he devoted himself to Wolfgang's musical education. A pushy father - but what would you do if you had WA as a son? Wolfgang had an elder sister, Maria Anna, who was also very musical.

Married: Maria Constanze Caecilia Josepha Johanna Aloysia Weber. Usually known as Constanze. This was another case of the wrong sister (see Haydn page 43). Mozart was originally in love with Constanze's sister. She wouldn't have him so he tried another sister, Josepha. No luck, and Constanze was his third choice. Despite this, they seem to have been very happy together.

Children: Six, but only two survived.

Jobs: Not very good at hanging on to jobs. He was sacked from a post at the court of the Archbishop of Salzburg with the help of a kick on the backside. Mozart did not like to be treated like a servant, and tact was not one of his strong points. He became a freelance musician, making money from composing, putting on series of concerts and giving music lessons.

HOP IT WOLFGANG!

Life's work: Most famous operas are *The Marriage of Figaro, Don Giovanni, Cosi fan Tutte, The Magic Flute*; 41 symphonies; 25 piano concertos; violin concertos; lots of string quartets and other chamber music; choral music written for church occasions including the famous *Requiem*.

Claim to fame: All the above. Mozart was a genius. Everyone says so.

TEST YOUR GENIUS POTENTIAL

Are you about to follow in Mozart's footsteps? Answer these simple questions to find out:

1. How many symphonies have you composed recently? (By the age of 14, Mozart had already written 12.)

2. How many instruments can you play? (Mozart played harpsichord, clavier, organ and violin by the time he was seven.)

3. Can you play the piano with a cloth across the keyboard? (Mozart could. This was one of his favourite party tricks at the age of about eight.)

4. Do you like the sound of the solo trumpet? (Mozart didn't. He didn't much like the flute either.)

5. How's your sense of humour? (Mozart's was unbelievably disgusting and rude!)

PAYING THE BILLS

Mozart was one of the first composers to manage without a patron. Actually, sometimes he and Constanze found it rather difficult to manage at all - neither of them were very good with money. In Vienna, Mozart organised several series of public concerts which at first were very successful. But, by 1789, Mozart found that there was very little interest in Vienna in his latest series of concerts. Luckily, his operas were more of a hit. Nevertheless Mozart ended up writing quite a few letters like this one:

...If you should find it inconvenient to part with so large a sum at once, then I beg you to lend me until tomorrow at least a couple of hundred gulden as ... I have to pay [my landlord] on the spot...

The Mozarts' money problems dogged them until the end of Wolfgang's life. After his death, Constanze got her act together and began to manage her finances rather better. She remarried, and lived happily and comfortably into old age. She never forgot her genius husband, though, continuing to call herself 'Widow Mozart'.

CLASSIC FORMS

An easy-reference guide to the kinds of words you find on the backs of CDs of music by Haydn and Mozart:

concerto (see also p.40) by Mozart's time, the concerto had become very popular because it gave a talented soloist the chance to show off. Mozart himself showed off brilliantly in his 25 piano concertos, particularly in bits called *cadenzas* where the soloist was left free to make the music up. Like symphonies (see opposite), concertos were made up of separate parts, called movements.

opera Mozart's operas mostly tell the stories of

everyday people and their servants, with a bit of magic thrown in here and there. They are full of action, all helped along by the fast-moving plot and music. No wonder they were such a hit then... and are now.

quartet the string quartet is made up of two violins, a viola and a cello. Both Haydn and Mozart wrote lots of string quartets. This kind of music is called chamber music because it is better suited to a chamber-kind-of-room rather than a large concert hall. There are lots of other combinations of instruments used in chamber music: the trio, the quintet, the sextet, the octet, the piano trio, the piano quartet, the piano quintet... (get the picture?)

symphony a piece written for full orchestra. A symphony usually has three or four separate parts or 'movements'. A symphony is full of contrasts - some fast bits, some slow bits, big climaxes and peaceful quiet bits. Haydn and Mozart dashed them off quite quickly. Lots of them have nicknames depending sometimes on where they were written *Paris, Linz, London*; or where they were first performed *Prague*; or who they were written for *Haffner*; or describing some characteristic of the music *Clock, Drum Roll, The Hen, Surprise*.

PLAYING TOGETHER ...AND ALONE

IT'S SO MUCH FUN TO PLAY TOGETHER ...

From the start of musical times people loved to play together...

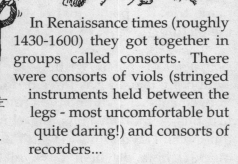

In Renaissance times (roughly 1430-1600) they got together in groups called consorts. There were consorts of viols (stringed instruments held between the legs - most uncomfortable but quite daring!) and consorts of recorders...

There were some people who just loved making a lot of noise on raucous instruments called shawms, as well as sackbuts and other blowy instruments. These instruments were often played outdoors for processions, or as the background music for parties and the like, because they were just too darned noisy inside!

In Baroque times (roughly 1600-1750), the idea of a balanced ensemble began to take shape.

By Classical times (roughly 1750-1827), the orchestra was beginning to shape up nicely.

By Romantic times (19th century) the orchestra was simply huge. Composers such as Berlioz (see page 64) and Wagner (see page 74) wrote music for ridiculously vast numbers of people...

In the 20th century people thought up new ways of playing together and it was just as much fun as it has always been...

MUSICAL INVENTIONS

Some musical instruments just quietly developed over hundreds of years into the instruments we play today. Others were invented and arrived on the scene with more of a splash!

piano Bartolomeo Cristofori (1655-1731) invented the fortepiano, which we now call the pianoforte (or piano). In actual fact, when Cristofori produced the first fortepiano in 1709 he called it a *gravicembalo col piano e forte* (harpsichord with soft and loud). The exciting thing about this new invention was that it could play both soft and loud because the strings were hit with hammers rather than being plucked as in a harpsichord.

saxophone invented by and named after Adolphe Sax (1814-94). A cross between a clarinet and a brass instrument it soon became popular with military bands, and was then taken up by jazz performers.

theremin invented by Léon Thérémin. An electrical instrument that makes an unearthly 'wowing' sound. The weird thing is that the player doesn't actually touch the theremin to play it - he or she simply waves their hands around it to alter pitch and volume.

Fender electric guitar Leo Fender (*b*.1909) invented and made the first guitar with a solid body. Where would pop and rock music be without him? The *Fender Stratocaster* (first sold in 1954) is a classic that still sells like hot cakes today.

IT'S EVEN MORE FUN PLAYING ON YOUR OWN ...
(BECAUSE YOU CAN SHOW OFF!)

Some people have always
liked showing off!

However, serious musical showing off really got going in the 19th century with the arrival of the *virtuoso*. A virtuoso is someone who is rather good at playing lots and lots of notes very fast and very brilliantly. To become a virtuoso takes a lot of practice - unless you are just naturally extremely talented that is!

VARIOUS VIRTUOSI

NICOLÒ PAGANINI
Born 1782, Genoa, Italy
Died 1840

Instrument: violin

Claim to fame: the first megastar virtuoso. Young Nicolò was forced to practise his violin all hours of the day and night by his father. Amazingly, this didn't put him off. Paganini went on to be violinist of such superhuman technical wizardry that people simply gasped and gaped in his presence and said things like 'inconceivable' and 'unbelievable'. Paganini also wrote music for the violin. Other violinists took one look at it and said that it was unplayable, but needless to say Paganini proved them wrong...

FRANZ LISZT
Born 1811, near Sopron, Hungary
Died 1886

Instrument: piano

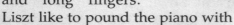

Claim to fame: shredded the piano keys with his incredible virtuosity, and long fingers.
Liszt like to pound the piano with an incredible ferocity. Piano-makers were forced to make stronger pianos just to protect their instruments from the maestro. In 1831 Liszt heard Paganini play in Paris. He was so stunned that he withdrew from public life for a while to... improve his piano playing. Liszt wrote fiendishly difficult piano music and specialised in arranging huge pieces for the piano, such as Berlioz's *Symphonie Fantastique*.

ANDRÉS SEGOVIA
Born 1893, Linares, Spain
Died 1987

Instrument: guitar

Claim to fame: the first guitar virtuoso. Segovia's family didn't want him to become a musician, but this boy was determined. He taught himself to play the guitar and developed his own technique. At the time, the guitar wasn't considered to be a 'serious' instrument - but

Segovia changed that. He rewrote music by Bach, Handel, Mozart etc. for the guitar. He commissioned composers to write new pieces for the guitar. And he played brilliantly, packing out concert halls over the world.

MUSICAL IMPROVEMENTS

Some instrument-makers are famous for their improvements to particular instruments.

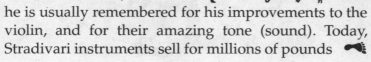

Stradivari Antonio Stradivari (1644-1737) made some of the greatest violins ever known. He also made violas and cellos, but he is usually remembered for his improvements to the violin, and for their amazing tone (sound). Today, Stradivari instruments sell for millions of pounds

Boehm Without Theobald Boehm (1794-1881) the flute would not be the instrument it is today. He made lots of improvements, changing the size and position of the fingerholes, and generally making the flute easier to play, as well as making it produce a bigger and better sound.

Dolmetsch Arnold Dolmetsch (1858-1940) became interested in old instruments which had fallen out of favour. One of these happened to be the recorder. He

---

 The Ashmolean Museum in Oxford has a great collection of Stradivarius instruments which you can go and look at.

made modern versions of Renaissance recorders and taught people how to play them, starting the recorder craze which still affects most British schools.

Heckel The Heckel family is famous for making bassoons. At the suggestion of Richard Wagner (see page 74), Wilhelm Heckel (1856-1909) also invented a new instrument called the heckelphone.

DEAFNESS AND ROMANCE

LUDWIG VAN BEETHOVEN

CURRICULUM VITAE
Born: 16 December 1770, Bonn, Germany
Died: 26 March 1827, Vienna, Austria

Parents: Johann and Maria Magdalena van Beethoven. Johann was determined that the young Ludwig should be a child prodigy like Mozart (pushy parents again!). He forced Ludwig to practise the piano, organ, violin and viola for hours on end, but Ludwig just wasn't the big child-hit that Johann was hoping for...

Biggest tragedy: the deafness which started to affect him around the age of 30. By 50 he was totally deaf. It didn't stop him composing but it did stop him performing.

Biggest put-down: 'There are and there will be thousands of princes. There is only one Beethoven.' (Spoken to one of his greatest fans, Prince Lichnowsky.)

Love life: always, apparently, in love with at least one woman but never managed to marry any of them.

Jobs: court musician in Bonn until 1792 when he moved to Vienna. Beethoven quickly became famous for his brilliant piano playing, and for his many musical talents. Unfortunately his deafness put an end to his piano playing career, and he turned more and more to writing music. Beethoven lived for the rest of his life off the money he made from the publication of his music.

Life's work: 9 symphonies; 5 piano concertos; string quartets and other chamber music; lots of solo piano music; the immense setting of the Mass called the *Missa Solemnis*; one opera *Fidelio*. Beethoven couldn't decide how to start this opera so it has 4 different overtures, Leonora 1, Leonora 2, Leonora 3 and the final version.

Prize for: most dramatic death scene in the whole history of music. Beethoven is lying on his death bed. Outside, there is snow on the ground. Suddenly a bolt of lightning fills the death chamber with a lurid light and there is a great crash of thunder. Beethoven lifts his right hand with clenched fist and makes one final, defiant gesture to the world, and then... dies.

'A SOMEWHAT SAVAGE ASPECT'

Beethoven's appearance was as dramatic as his music: 'Beethoven could not have been much more than 5 feet

4 inches tall... His body was thick-set; his head was unusually large, covered with long, unkempt, almost completely grey hair, giving him a somewhat savage aspect... His forehead was high and broad, his brown eyes small, almost retreating into his head when he laughed. They could, however, suddenly become unusually prominent and large, with rolling or flashing - the pupils always turned upwards - or not moving at all, staring fixedly ahead... His mouth was well formed, the lips even, the nose rather broad. His laughter... often burst out immoderately... the huge head would swell, the face become still broader, and the whole effect was not seldom that of a grimacing caricature...'

BEETHOVEN: THE SYMPHONIES

As everyone knows, Beethoven wrote nine symphonies. Here is a quick 'what they don't tell you about' guide to Beethoven's sensational stunners:

SYMPHONY NO 1: C MAJOR

Beethoven's first symphonic attempt was performed for the first time on 2 April 1800 in Vienna. People liked it. One critic wrote that it was 'a symphony which revealed much art, novelty and wealth of ideas.' Listen out for the wind section (flutes, oboes, clarinets, bassoons) in this symphony. Beethoven uses them a lot. The critic wasn't so keen on this: '...there was too much use of wind instruments, so that it sounded more like a wind-band than an orchestra.'

Symphony no 2: D major

Composed in 1801-2. Also got a good review: 'a work full of new and original ideas, of great vigour, effective instrumentation and erudite development.' Erudite means clever in a sort of clever-clever sort of way. That's the sort of person Beethoven was.

Symphony no 3: E flat major

Called the *Eroica*. This one really set the cat among the pigeons! For a start it was nearly twice as long as any symphony written before. And it was much more complicated. People found it very tricky to understand: 'This long, extremely difficult composition is actually a very long drawn-out, daring and wild fantasy.' And this was one of the good reviews.

As Beethoven was writing this symphony he fully intended to dedicate it to Napoleon. He saw Napoleon as a hero who was setting free the oppressed French people and giving them some 'Fraternity, Liberty and Equality'. Beethoven was very keen on this sort of thing. Then Beethoven received the news that Napoleon had made himself Emperor of France. So much for fraternity etc., this man was obviously a tyrant! Beethoven tore off the title page and threw it on the floor. Instead the symphony was given the title *Eroica* - the 'heroic symphony'.

SYMPHONY NO 4: B FLAT MAJOR

Beethoven worked on this jolly number at the same time as he was composing the 5th symphony, which is anything but jolly. Cleverly, he managed not to confuse the two.

SYMPHONY NO 5: C MINOR

You know this one. It starts da - da - da - daa. These four notes were described as 'fate knocking at the door'. Heavy stuff. The da-da-da-daa tune appears throughout the symphony in different disguises.

SYMPHONY NO 6: F MAJOR THE *PASTORAL*.

The 5th and 6th symphonies were both given their first performance in an epic concert in Vienna on 22 December 1808 (the concert also included a piano concerto and some other music just in case it wasn't quite long enough). The *Pastoral* symphony was inspired by Beethoven's holidays in the countryside. Each movement has a title: 'Merrymaking of the Peasants'; 'Storm'; 'Thankful feelings after the storm' - that sort of thing. In 'Scene by the brook' you can hear the song of a nightingale (played by the flute), the quail (oboe) and cuckoo (clarinet).

SYMPHONY NO 7: A MAJOR

This symphony was such a success that the audience demanded an instant repetition of the slow movement. They loved it! There is lots and lots of rhythm in this symphony - you could dance to the last movement.

SYMPHONY NO 8: F MAJOR

Smaller-scale but no less perfect than any of the others.

SYMPHONY NO 9: D MINOR THE CHORAL.

Called the *Choral* because it has four soloists and a choir in its last movement. Beethoven was now experimenting wildly. He was also completely deaf, so all this amazing music was composed inside his head. Being deaf made conducting very difficult, but Beethoven insisted on conducting the first performance on 7 May 1824. At the end of the symphony, one of the soloists had to pull the great composer's sleeve to point out that everyone was applauding wildly. Lost in his own deaf world, he just hadn't noticed.

AND SYMPHONY NO 10

The last music Beethoven wrote before he died was some sketches for a 10th symphony. But the actual sound of Beethoven's 10th was in his head and went with him to the grave...

THE VERY ROMANTIC LIFE OF HECTOR BERLIOZ

Berlioz was born in 1803, the year that Beethoven was writing his *Eroica* symphony. This is very appropriate because Berlioz saw himself as a bit of a Romantic hero. He was the son of a doctor, and his father was determined that Hector should follow in his footsteps. He actually prevented Hector from learning the piano! But Hector was more interested in music than medical school. After a lot of rows, his father finally gave in and allowed Hector to become a composer. Hector's other big passion in life was women. He was always madly, passionately and deeply in love with someone:

HECTOR'S DIARY OF LOVE

1815 Meylan: Holiday Romance
I am so in love. Her name is Estelle. The first moment I saw her, I felt a shock of electricity buzz through my body. I love her. She is tall with beautiful eyes. She wears pink, lace-up boots.

1827 Paris: Shakespearian Romance
I am so in love. Her name is Harriet Smithson. She is an Irish actress, and she plays all the great Shakespearian roles - Ophelia, Juliet, Desdemona. She is my Ophelia, my Juliet, my Desdemona. I have lost the power of sleep, my innermost thoughts are all of Harriet, Harriet, Harriet... She shall be my wife, and I shall write my grandest symphony...

1830 Paris: Musical Romance
I am so in love. Her name is Camille Moke. She is a pianist. She has superb black hair and large blue eyes which sometimes sparkle like stars. Her smile is like the sun breaking through the fog. I have dared to ask her to marry me! We are engaged...

1831 Florence: Cruelly Betrayed!
My beloved is married to another! She has broken our engagement!! I will go to Paris, I will murder them all, and then I shall shoot myself!!!

1833 Paris: Harriet Again

I have finally met my most beloved Harriet. Our families disapprove but we shall marry. She reproaches me and says I do not love her. I drink poison before her very eyes and declare that I have never loved anyone else but her. (Am very sick afterwards but it was worth it.)

1842 Brussels: The Reality of Marriage

My wife is a nag, and is insanely jealous of my every move. I am in Brussels with Marie Recio, a singer with a voice like a cat...

1854 Paris: And Finally

Harriet dead. I cannot be but sad, for her beauty was gone and her health ruined by drink. I will marry Marie, it is my duty.

MUSICAL INSPIRATION

Berlioz's fixation with Harriet Smithson inspired some of his most passionate music, particularly the amazing 'Fantastic Symphony' (*Symphonie Fantastique*). Harriet appears throughout this symphony as 'the beloved' in the form of a short musical tune called the *idée fixe* (fixed idea). Berlioz uses the *idée fixe* in different ways in each movement.

LIEDERS OF THE PACK

Some people have trouble remembering the difference between Schubert and Schumann, probably because they both wrote lots of *lieder* (see below). However, you will have no problem after reading this easy guide to the two Ss.

FRANZ PETER SCHUBERT

Born: 31 January 1797, Vienna

Youthful passions: music. In 1808 he became a chorister at the Imperial Chapel in Vienna. He was already composing songs, string quartets and piano pieces.

Marriage: never married, but was at various times in love with soprano Thérèse Grob, and with his pupil Caroline Esterhazy.

Appearance: short (about 5 feet) with a head rather big for his body. Plumpish. Very short-sighted so wore round glasses. Brown, curly hair, and bushy eyebrows.

Music: 9 symphonies, 17 or so operas, lots of chamber music and more than 600 lieder.

Fame: surprisingly, Schubert was not well-known in his own lifetime. He wasn't a virtuoso like Mozart or Beethoven, and his music was not widely performed. However, he had a circle of very loyal and admiring friends who held musical parties to hear Schubert's music. These became known as *Schubertiads*.

The end: died tragically young of a horrible disease in 1828.

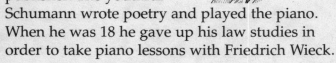

SPOT THE DIFFERENCE

ROBERT SCHUMANN

Born: 8 June 1810, Zwickau, Saxony

Youthful passions: music and literature. His father was a bookseller and publisher. The youthful Schumann wrote poetry and played the piano. When he was 18 he gave up his law studies in order to take piano lessons with Friedrich Wieck.

Marriage: you could write a whole book about Schumann's love life (people have!). He fell in love with Friedrich Wieck's daughter, Clara. It took the two lovers five years to persuade Friedrich to allow them to marry. The father thought that Schumann was a drunkard and good-for-nothing and not worthy of his talented daughter (more about her on page 71). Schumann had other loves too. Before getting serious about Clara he was engaged to Ernestine von Fricken, a rich heiress. Well, that's what she told Schumann! In fact she was adopted and therefore not an heiress at all. Schumann quickly wriggled out of the engagement when he found out.

Appearance: taller than Schubert, straight dark hair, no glasses, rather piercing eyes.

Music: piano music including a piano concerto, 4 symphonies, chamber music and more than 250 lieder.

Fame: Schumann might have had a career as a concert pianist but for two things: he was never going to be as good a pianist as his wife, and an injury to his hand. Cures including baths in cow dung and herbal bandages had little effect... Instead he became a highly successful composer and music critic.

The end: Schumann went mad. He spent his last years in an asylum where he died in 1856.

LIEDER REVEALED

So what are these mysterious lieder and what do you do with them? The short answer is 'songs' and you sing them with someone playing a piano accompaniment. (The German word for one song is 'lied', lots of songs 'lieder'.) Of course, composers had been writing songs for centuries, but the 19th century was a particularly good time for lieder. German poets such as Goethe and Schiller were writing poems that just cried out to be set to music. Both Schubert and Schumann were masters of expressing the meaning of the words through their music, bringing the words of the poetry alive.

Schubert and Schumann both wrote music for groups of songs, known as song cycles. These are about wandering millers, winter journeys, babbling brooks, rustling forests, but most of all - love. Sometimes things get a bit terrifying with the appearance of ghosts, ghouls and death itself.

THE GHOSTLY DOUBLE (SCHUBERT)

'The night is still, the streets are hushed; in this house once lived my beloved. Though she left town long ago, the house still stands in the very same place. A man is standing there too, looking up and wringing his hands in pain. I shudder when I see his face - for the face I see in the moonlight is my own! You ghostly double, ghastly fellow, why do you mock the pain of love that tortured me in this very place, many a night in times gone by?'

CLARA SCHUMANN

Before Clara was even born her father had already decided that she would be a concert pianist. Clara didn't have much say in the matter. She had several piano lessons every day. In between piano lessons she practised... the piano. She played her first piano concerto in public when she was nine. Wherever she went, her father went too, watching carefully over his star pupil.

When Robert Schumann came to live as a pupil in Friedrich Wieck's house, Clara was only 11 years old. For her it was like having an elder brother. For Robert, it must have been difficult not to be jealous of this 11-year-old who played the piano brilliantly, much more brilliantly than him...

Robert and Clara declared their love for each other in 1835. Friedrich was not happy. He tried everything. He sent Clara away. He threatened to shoot Schumann. He banned him from entering his house. He opened all of Clara's mail. He refused to let her go out alone. He was absolutely determined that Clara was going to be a concert pianist and not a housewife!

Of course, it didn't work. In the end, Schumann took Wieck to court and won permission to marry Clara. They were married on 12 September 1840.

Pianist and housewife

Some of Wieck's concerns turned out to be justified. Within only a few months of getting married Clara was already complaining that she had not been able to practise her beloved piano because she could not disturb her husband when he was composing. But later that year she went on tour to Copenhagen and soon Schumann knew what it felt like to be introduced to people as 'the pianist's husband'!

Clara and Robert had eight children (although one died soon after birth). Clara still managed to tour all over Europe - to Russia and to Britain where she played to Queen Victoria. (Queen V. apparently talked throughout Clara's performance.) When Robert became ill, Clara was even busier, touring and playing to earn enough money to provide for her sick husband and large family. She was not allowed to visit her husband once he went into the asylum, and did not see him for over two years. But when she received a telegram saying 'If you want to see your husband alive, come with all haste,' she rushed to his side. He died two days later. Clara lived on for another forty years.

ROMANCE AT THE OPERA

TRAGIC TALES

When Monteverdi wrote his opera *Orfeo* he changed the ending of the story so that his opera would end happily. Romantic opera composers (that is, composers from the Romantic period), however, had absolutely no problems with sad endings. Tragic heroes and heroines litter their operas, going mad, throwing themselves off tall towers, dying of terrible diseases, being murdered on and off stage. If you feel like a good weep - there's nothing better than a Romantic opera.

TOP TRAGEDY

GIOACCHINO ROSSINI

1792-1868, Italian. Most people think of Rossini as a composer of light-hearted, frothy operas such as *The Barber of Seville* and *Cinderella*. But he could turn his hand to a bit of tragedy when the occasion arose. His *Ermione* has love, madness, blood-spattered daggers and at least two corpses at the end. He also continued the trend for operas based on historical subjects such as *Elisabetta, Regina d'Inghilterra* (Elizabeth, Queen of England).

GAETANO DONIZETTI

1797-1848, Italian. Donizetti was so excited by *Elisabetta, Regina d'Inghilterra* that he decided to continue in the same vein... He wrote operas about Anne Boleyn, Mary Queen of Scots, and his own version of Queen Elizabeth. He managed to combine history and tragedy in *Lucia di Lammermoor* which was based on a story by Sir Walter Scott. Lucia goes mad, so if you want to sound knowledgeable about this opera, just talk about 'the famous mad scene' and everyone will be very impressed.

RICHARD WAGNER

1813-83, German. Wagner spent pretty well the whole of his life writing operas. He even built his own opera house, in Bayreuth. The first works to be staged there were the four operas of *The Ring of the Nibelungen*, in 1876. (Just so you know the four operas are: *The Rhinegold, The Valkyrie, Siegfried* and *Twilight of the Gods*.) Tchaikovsky went to the first Festival at Bayreuth, but he didn't think much of Wagner's masterpiece, remarking that it was 'absolute nonsense, from a musical point of view'...

GUISEPPI VERDI

1813-1901, Italian. Born the same year as Wagner, but there the similarities end. Verdi wrote one or two comic operas (notably *Falstaff*), but he was really very, very good at tragedy. In *La Traviata*, the heroine of the piece, Violetta, dies of a wasting disease called consumption. It takes the whole of the last act for her to finally peg out. Unfortunately, at the first performance the soprano singing the part of Violetta looked rather too healthy and fat to be believable and the audience just rolled around laughing every time she opened her mouth. As soon as Verdi got in a sickly soprano, the opera was a huge success.

GEORGES BIZET

1838-75, French. Bizet is really only remembered today for one opera, *Carmen*, although he did write others. *Carmen* shocked people when it was first staged in 1875 because they thought the subject matter was scandalous (gypsies, smugglers etc). As usual, the heroine dies at the end of the opera, but this time there is no long, drawn-out death scene, just a brief and rather brutal stabbing.

PYOTR TCHAIKOVSKY

1840-93, Russian. Tchaikovsky is better known for his splashy, dramatic orchestral music, and his ballet music (*Sleeping Beauty*, *The Nutcracker*). But he was a real fan of Mozart's operas, and of Bizet's *Carmen* (as we know, he wasn't so keen on Wagner). His most famous opera is *Eugene Onegin*. This time the heroine, Tatyana, doesn't die, but she does marry the wrong man. If you want to sound knowledgeable about this opera, just mention the 'letter scene' (when Tatyana writes of her love for Onegin).

GIACOMO PUCCINI

1858-1924, Italian. Wrote *Manon Lescaut*, *La Bohème*, *Tosca*, *Madame Butterfly*, *Turandot* - all guaranteed to send you from the theatre weeping into your hankie! Puccini was very good at endings - the heroine dies (from consumption in *La Bohème*, jumps off a tower in Tosca, stabs herself in *Madame Butterfly*, from sheer exhaustion in *Manon Lescaut*) - a few dramatic chords - and the curtain falls.

RICHARD STRAUSS

1864-1949, German. Much to his friends' astonishment, Strauss married a singer called Pauline de Ahna who bullied and nagged him throughout his life. Strauss suffered his wife's scenes with

good humour but got his own back by writing an opera about their marriage - *Intermezzo*. The sets for the first production were copied from Strauss's own house, and Strauss even invited the leading lady to meet the terrible Pauline so that she could reproduce her moods and tempers on stage. Strauss was also good at tragedy (*Elektra*), and brilliant at writing very high and very beautiful music for three sopranos (*Der Rosenkavalier*) who all end the opera alive!

A NIGHT AT THE OPERA

LA BOHÈME BY GIACOMO PUCCINI

1. Scene: a freezing attic in Paris on Christmas Eve. Rodolfo is a poet and he lives with three other arty friends, a musician, a philosopher and an artist. Rodolfo bumps into his next-door neighbour, Mimi. She coughs painfully and he says 'Your tiny hand is frozen'. They fall in love (in a big way).

2. Scene: Christmas Eve in the Latin Quarter. Mimi and Rodolfo stroll out to meet their friends. Marcello (the artist) is reunited with an old flame - Musetta, a real flirt!

3. Scene: outside a tavern where Marcello and Musetta are now living. A cold, snowy February evening. Mimi comes to see Marcello to ask his advice. Rodolfo is insanely jealous of her every move. But we discover that Rodolfo is tortured by the thought of Mimi's failing health and that he can do nothing to help her. The two agree to part.

4. Scene: the attic again. Marcello and Rodolfo are gossiping, laughing and playing around. A knock interrupts their fun. It is Musetta with Mimi who is very ill. Rodolfo and Mimi are reunited, and Mimi dies. Rodolfo sobs a final 'Mimi' and the curtain falls. The audience weeps.

WHERE HAVE ALL THE WOMEN GONE?

Have you ever noticed that musical stories are usually about men? If you look through most books about music you might start to wonder whether any women ever played any instruments, or sang a note, or wrote down any music, or in fact had any part in the story of music at all. So here are the bits they don't usually tell you about the story of music... from the women's point of view.

KEEPING SILENCE

In the beginning, as the Christian church was getting up and running, men and women sang together in praise of God and no one saw anything wrong with that. But as the Church began to get more organised, the men in charge began to mutter things like 'women should keep silence in the churches' (quotation from the Bible, 1 Corinthians, Chapter 14, Verse 34). Then they set up special choirs such as the Schola Cantorum (see page 11) which were for boys and men only.

However, women continued to sing God's praises... in convents. Most nuns learned the basics of reading and singing. They often sang their way through nine services every day! Nuns also composed music for Christian services and although much of this music has been forgotten or lost over the centuries, one or two famous names have survived to the present day. Perhaps the most famous of all is Hildegard of Bingen.

HILDEGARD THE DREAMER

Hildegard of Bingen (1098-1179) established a new convent at Rupertsberg near Bingen in Germany between 1147 and 1150. She continued as abbess there until her death. If St Gregory got his inspiration from a dove (see page 11), Hildegard got hers through visions. She wrote works about medical and religious matters, and she composed music for services in the convent. All of this came to her as if in a dream. Hildegard collected together her compositions into a large work called *Symphony of the Harmony of Heavenly Revelations*, a suitably dreamy title!

TROUVÈRES AND TROBAIRITZ

Courtly musicians were all the rage during the 12th and 13th centuries in France. In the south of France noble musicians were usually known as *trouvères* if they were men (see page 17), and *trobairitz* if they were women. Whether you were a trouvère or a trobairitz didn't make much difference to the subject matter of your songs, however! They were about love, usually when it's not going well. Here's a typical example:

> *I must sing of that which I would rather not:*
> *I am so angry with someone who is my friend.*
> *I love him more than anything,*
> *But pity and kindness don't seem to do any good,*
> *Nor do my beauty, my worth or my wits:*
> *I am tricked and betrayed*
> *Just as if I was ugly!*

LEARNING HOW TO BE A HOUSEWIFE

One of the problems for women over the next few centuries was that no one expected them to do anything but either a) get married or b) go into a convent. Wanting to be a hairdresser/ rocket scientist/ astronaut/ librarian/ pilot just wasn't allowed. The  good news was that people thought that it was a great idea for girls to learn some music, how to play an instrument, how to sing nicely etc. The bad news was that they were not usually permitted to perform outside their own homes. So history is stuffed full of talented amateur women musicians, all playing dutifully to their husbands and a small circle of friends, but we know very little about them.

Of course, there were exceptions. Women singers began to be in demand as opera became more popular. The opera composer Giulio Caccini (see page 27) taught his two talented daughters how to sing in the new dramatic style, and both women held professional singing posts in the Medici court in Florence. Another talented daughter was Barbara Strozzi. Her father was a poet who worked with Claudio Monteverdi on his operas. Barbara was a singer, but she was also a composer and many of her compositions were published.

INSTRUMENTS SUITABLE FOR FEMALES

People continued to have very definite ideas about what was and what was not suitable for a female musician. Fanny Mendelssohn was the older sister of the famous composer Felix Mendelssohn. Both Fanny and Felix were talented musicians, and both were given a good musical training. But Fanny was forbidden by her father from performing in public or publishing most of her compositions. Meanwhile, Felix was given help and encouragement by his father and sister and soon found fame and fortune. When Fanny did have songs published... most of them were under her brother's name.

The definite ideas even extended to what instruments a woman should play. Women were allowed to be singers and pianists and they could also play the harp because it was a graceful and feminine instrument. However, playing a stringed instrument such as the violin or, (even worse!) the cello, was considered very unfeminine. This situation began to change at the beginning of the 19th century, but outlandish instruments such as the clarinet or the trumpet were still considered quite unsuitable for women ...

JOBS FOR THE GIRLS

By the beginning of the 20th century women could learn to play virtually any instrument they wanted, and they could go to music college to study their instrument. But they couldn't play in most of the professional orchestras around the world because... they were all male! In the USA, many women musicians got so fed up with this that they set up their own, women's orchestras. From the 1920s to the 1940s there were about thirty women's orchestras in the USA. Even more ground breaking was the fact that they were often conducted by women, too.

NAMES TO REMEMBER

Next time you read a book about music, look out for these names. Even better, listen out for their music.

CÉCILE CHAMINADE

Born: Paris, France 1857
Died: 1944

Early life: both parents were keen on music, and her mother taught her to play the piano. Cécile wanted to attend a music school, the Paris Conservatoire, but her father would not permit it. However, he did allow her to take private piano and composition lessons.

Music: she became most celebrated for her piano works. After 1890 she started a career as a concert pianist, playing her own compositions. She was especially popular in the USA.

ETHEL SMYTH

Born: London, UK, 1858
Died: 1944

COME ON ETHEL

Early life: decided early on that she wanted to study music, but met with opposition from her father who did not want his daughter to become a professional musician. Ethel went on strike, refusing to go to church, ride her horse, sing or play the piano. Eventually her father gave in and she went to study in Leipzig.

Music: her most famous work is her opera *The Wreckers*. It is set in Cornwall and is a tragic tale of two lovers who defy the rest of their village, and are eventually left to drown in a cave. Ethel also fought for the right to vote for women, and wrote the suffragette song *The March of the Women*.

AMY BEACH

Born: New Hampshire, USA 1867
Died: 1944
Early life: was playing the piano and composing pieces by the age of four. Launched on a career as a concert pianist, but gave it up when she married at the age of 18.

Music: luckily Dr Henry Harris Aubrey Beach (her husband) encouraged his gifted wife to carry on composing. She wrote lots of songs, piano pieces, and the *Gaelic* symphony. Like Messiaen (see page 87), she was interested in birdsong, and spent hours writing down the music of bird calls.

NAMES TO LOOK OUT FOR...

Look out for the music of these women composers who have made their names during the 20th century, and many of whom are still writing today...

ELIZABETH POSTON
ELISABETH LUTYENS
ELIZABETH MACONCHY
JUDITH BINGHAM
IMOGEN HOLST
NICOLA LEFANU
HILARY TANN
THEA MUSGRAVE
JUDITH WEIR
DIANA BURRELL
SOFIA GUBAIDULINA
RUTH CRAWFORD SEEGER

NEW DIRECTIONS

THE FUTURE →

ANYTHING GOES

A whirlwind of ideas hit music in the 20th century. New was in - new influences, new instruments, new sounds, new rhythms, new ways to use old instruments - if it was new it was cool. As usual, many people found all this newness rather terrifying. As the British composer Vaughan Williams remarked after conducting a performance of his own 4th symphony: 'Well if that's modern music, I don't like it.'

RITE ON RHYTHMS

The most famous of all outraged audiences was the one that attended the first night of the ballet the *Rite of Spring*. The music was by Igor Stravinsky (1882-1971) and the dance was by Diaghilev and Nijinsky and the audience absolutely hated it!

Over ten years later, the *Rite of Spring* was still upsetting people:

> *Who wrote this fiendish 'Rite of Spring',*
> *What right had he to write the thing,*
> *Against our helpless ears to fling*
> *Its crash, crash, cling, clang, bing, bang, bing?*

What was so exciting and new about Stravinsky's music?

The answer is: rhythm.

Up to 1913, most Western music was written in quite regular rhythms, such as:

1 2, 1 2, 1 2, 1 2, 1 2, 1 2 etc. (marching rhythm)

or 1 2 3, 1 2 3, 1 2 3, 1 2 3, 1 2 3 etc. (waltzing rhythm)

or 1 2 3 4, 1 2 3 4, 1 2 3 4, 1 2 3 4 etc. (a nice, straightforward, common rhythm)

Stravinsky decided to break out of these regular rhythms, and in the *Rite of Spring* he goes wild with rhythm. You try dancing to this!:

1 2 3, 1 2 3 4, 1 2 3, 1 2 3 4, 1 2 3 4 5, 1 2 3 4 etc.

FUNNY FOLK

Another big idea for composers in the 20th century was to look for inspiration in new places. Some composers became interested in the music of other cultures - Indian music, music of the East and of Africa. Others got interested in something closer to home - folk music. Folk music is usually described as music that isn't written down, but is learned and passed on from one generation to the next. The kind of folk music changes from one region to the next: in Spain the local people may sing dramatic songs about bulls and bull-fights; in France they may sing you sloshed songs about wine; in most places there are songs about harvest time, or love, or death etc. etc.

Some composers got so keen on folk music that they decided to travel around the countryside collecting folk tunes. Funnily enough, these folk tunes sometimes worked their way into a composer's music. Or sometimes it wasn't even the tune itself, but just a kind of folky feeling...

TRAVELS OF THE FOLK COLLECTORS

BÉLA BARTÓK (1881-1945)
Hungarian
Worked with another Hungarian composer, Zoltán Kodály to collect folksong. The two composers travelled from village to village persuading the local people to sing into their portable recording machine. Later, Bartók became interested in folk music from many other countries including Romania, Turkey and North Africa. By the end of his life he had collected over 10,000 tunes. Bartók didn't often use folk tunes themselves, but you can hear the sounds and feel the feel of folk music in nearly all of his music.

RALPH VAUGHAN WILLIAMS (1872-1958)
British
Like Bartók, worked with another composer, Gustav Holst, to collect folksongs from around the British Isles. Vaughan Williams arranged some of the folk

songs he collected for voices. He was also quite good at writing 'original' folk tunes that sounded as if they had been around for centuries...

TRAVELS FURTHER AFIELD

Exotic music from far-flung countries excited two French composers, who both used the new sounds they heard to create their own unmistakeable music.

CLAUDE DEBUSSY (1862-1918)
French
In 1889, Debussy went to the World Exhibition in Paris and heard for the first time a Javanese gamelan orchestra. This is a traditional Indonesian orchestra made up of about twenty different instruments including tuned gongs, xylophones and drums. The sound of the gamelan was quite unlike anything that Debussy had ever heard before, and this sound soon found its way into his music.

OLIVIER MESSIAEN (1908-92)
French
Messiaen also became interested in the sounds of Eastern music, and he expanded the traditional Western orchestra with percussion instruments such as sets of gongs, wood blocks and Chinese cymbals. Messiaen was also fascinated by the sound of birdsong. He spent many hours in the French countryside noting  down the songs of particular birds. These birds pop up all over his music, but especially in the *Oiseaux Exotiques* (Exotic birds) for piano, wind and percussion.

HOW TO PREPARE A PIANO

If some composers went out of their way to use new, exotic instruments, other composers got new and exotic sounds out of old, well-known instruments. When an American composer, John Cage (1912-92), was asked to write some music to accompany a dance he wanted to use percussion instruments. The problem was that there was no room in the theatre where the dance was to be staged for lots of percussion. In fact, there was only space for one piano. So Cage made a percussion instrument out of the piano.

DO NOT TRY THIS AT HOME!

Cage changed the sound of the piano by attaching objects to the strings inside the piano itself. Different objects created different effects.

Ingredients for one prepared piano

Screws and bolts for metal, gong sounds
Washers and nuts for rattly, tambouriny sounds
Coins for more gong-like sounds
Pieces of rubber for flat sounds like a wood block
Plastic spoons for plastic spoon sounds

Attach to strings in specified positions and play one of Cage's pieces for prepared piano, for example *Bacchanale* or *The Perilous Night*.

HPSCHD
by John Cage and Lejaren Hiller

Take 51 tapes of harpsichord-type sounds and seven real-live harpsichords. The tapes are 20 minutes long and can be played in any order, on their own or together. Some of the live harpsichord players throw dice to select what music they should play and in what order. One of the harpsichord players plays any piece by W.A. Mozart.

The first performance of *HPSCHD* lasted for several hours and played to over 7000 people. During the performance, films and slides were projected on to huge screens around the hall.

PLAY IT YOURSELF: 4'33"

Here is your chance to perform a piece by John Cage. It's called *4 minutes 33 seconds* (written 4'33"). Here is what you do.

1. You will need an instrument - anything will do, recorder, piano, tambourine, marimba...
2. Invite an audience.
3. Walk on to the concert platform (the front room) in front of your audience (your mum and dad).
4. Hold your instrument, or stand in front of it in

silence for exactly *4'33"*. (To be absolutely exact you should know that the first movement of this piece lasts 30", the second movement 2'23" and the last movement 1'40". You might like to put this in your programme notes for your audience.)

5. At the end of 4'33" bow and await the wild applause for your virtuoso performance from your audience.

And the point of all this is?? Cage was quite serious when he wrote 4'33". He said that music could be any sound, even the sound of silence. Because in actual fact even silence has its own sound. Try it and see! If you sit in silence for four minutes what do you hear? Cars, voices talking, the dog barking, even the sound of your own blood pumping around your body?

NEW SOUNDS WITH NEW INSTRUMENTS

Not content with using old instruments or introducing unusual ones, some people went even further and started inventing completely new instruments that made some weird sounds! Theremin invented the *theremin* (see page 54) and Maurice Martenot invented another outlandish electric instrument called the *ondes martenot*. The ondes martenot has a keyboard so that the player can sound individual notes. It also has a ring on a ribbon so that the player can swoop up and down making truly unearthly 'Clanger'-like sounds. Messiaen loved the sound of the ondes martenot and you can hear it at its best in his huge *Turangalîla* symphony.

CONCRETE MUSIC

Nothing to do with cement or buildings!

Concrete music is made from recordings of everyday sounds such as a car, or someone laughing, or a cow mooing. The composer then plays around with these recordings to create a whole new sound-world. If you have the right equipment it's amazing what you can do to recorded sound! You can slow it down or speed it up; you can play it backwards; you can chop it up and put it back together again in a different order; you can make it into short bursts of sound and then play these bursts over and over again; you can record one sound on top of another sound; you can make the sound more wobbly; you can make it less wobbly...

A German composer, Karlheinz Stockhausen (*b*.1928) was into concrete music. He recorded the voice of one boy speaking and singing. He then played around with this recording until it sounded like a thousand different voices doing a thousand different things. This piece is called *Gesang der Jünglinge* (Song of the Youths).

SYNTHESIZED SOUND

With a synthesizer you can create almost any sound you can possibly think of. Synthesizers produce sound electronically. These days, if you have a MIDI (that's

Musical Instrument Digital Interface to you) keyboard and a computer you can do all sorts of exciting things. Throw in a sequencer and your synthesizer will remember any tune you care to throw at it and then repeat it back to you endlessly. You can multitrack (put together different lines of music). Add a sampler and you can sample (record) any sound and then do whatever you like to it. Synthesizers and computers are just GREAT for trying out all your wickedest musical ideas.

JAZZING IT UP

While Bach was busy beavering and Handel was harmonising and Mozart was writing melifluous melodies and Schubert was songwriting - the whole time that the story of Western music (as told in this book) was developing there was another story unfolding - of work songs and ballads and sea shanties and songs for entertainment and folk songs and all the other kinds of popular music. A lot of this music was never written down.

Then in 1877 Thomas Alva Edison invented the phonograph. For the first time live sound could be recorded and played back. The phonograph led to the gramophone, then (much later) the cassette tape, then (even later) the CD player. Today you can listen to your favourite music whenever you want to simply by putting a CD on, or by turning on the radio. Because of recording and broadcasting popular music in the 20th century has become BIG business...

So where and how did it all start?

JAZZ BEGINNINGS

The beginnings of jazz music grew out of a terrible trade in humans. Between the 16th and the 19th centuries millions of African people were forced to leave their homes and taken by ship across the Atlantic Ocean to work as slaves on plantations in America. Those who survived the appalling conditions on board ship found themselves in a strange land, parted from their family and friends, and forced to work long hours doing back-breaking tasks.

What could these newly enslaved people take with them? One of the few things they could take and pass on was... their music. Over many years a whole new mixture of musical traditions grew up. Some of the ingredients of this mixture were:

the different African traditions brought by enslaved people from many different regions of Africa
the European musical traditions brought by the Europeans who colonised America
and some of the results were:

call-and-response. You can try this with a friend. You sing a line:
"I'm a teapot" response "You're a teapot"
"I'm a saucer" response "You're a saucer"
"I'm a ..." get the idea?
Call-and-response was used by the slaves as they worked, with a leader singing out the call and a whole chorus responding. It was used in churches too, and it came to be an important part of Gospel music.

the Blues. Music full of 'blue' slightly off-pitch notes which tend to tug at the heart strings. The Blues told the stories of the sorrows of enslaved Africans, although the Blues wasn't actually called the Blues until the end of the 19th century.

Ragtime. Surfaced around the same time as the Blues. Style of piano music based on African-type rhythms using syncopation (accenting the 'weak' beats of the bar).

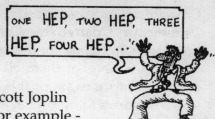

'ONE HEP, TWO HEP, THREE HEP, FOUR HEP...'

Just play or listen to a Scott Joplin piece - *The Entertainer* for example - and you'll soon hear exactly what syncopation is!

JAZZ QUOTES

'A jazz musician is a juggler who uses harmonies instead of oranges.'
Benny Green

'What they call jazz is just the music of people's emotions.'
Willie 'the Lion' Smith

JAZZ HOTSPOTS

New Orleans: where jazz started.
In the 19th century New Orleans was just heaving with music - operas, symphonies, marching bands for parades and funerals, music at parties and picnics, pianists in bars, music in the churches. Classic New Orleans instruments included clarinet, cornet, trombone, tuba, drums and banjo - all easily played on the march as the parades swung through the streets.

Chicago: where jazz moved to in the early part of the 20th century. Many New Orleans jazz players move north (new horizons: more money) including probably the most famous of them all - Louis Armstrong (see opposite for more about this jazz 'great'). Armstrong was a trumpeter - and what a trumpeter! He virtually invented the art of jazz improvisation (making it up as you go along). Jazz fans began to flock to Chicago to hear this trumpeting triumph.

New York: another jazz 'great', Duke Ellington, thrilled New Yorkers in the late 1920s and early '30s at the Cotton Club (more about him on page 98). Then came the Depression of the 1930s and many jazz musicians found themselves out of work. Then Benny Goodman came along and started the swing era.

TEST YOUR JAZZ KNOWLEDGE

Can you match these famous jazz players with the type of jazz that they made their own?

a Swing   1 Miles Davis
b Bebop   2 John Coltrane
c Cool   3 Benny Goodman
d Free jazz   4 Keith Jarrett
e Fusion   5 Charlie Parker

Answers (a3; b5; c1; d2; e4.)

People have been improvising for centuries. Bach did it the whole time. So did Mozart. But the problem with improvised music is that it's made up on the spot and then gone - so we don't know what Bach's and Mozart's improvisations sounded like. Luckily for us, Louis Armstrong's trumpet improvisations have been caught on record.

Top Ten Jazz Greats

Jelly Roll Morton

(Ferdinand La Menthe)
Born: 20 September 1885,
Gulfport, Mississippi
Died: 10 July 1941
Instrument: piano
Early life: came from a Creole (mixed race) family.
Became a gambler and played the piano as a sideline.

Claim to fame: Jelly cut some great records with his
band the *Red Hot Peppers*. When these records made
him lots of money Jelly bought the odd Cadillac or two
and had a large diamond set into his front tooth.

Music: Loosened up Ragtime and gave jazz its own
identity.

Louis Armstrong

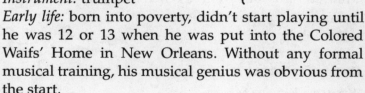

Born: 4 July 1900, New Orleans
Died: 6 July 1971
Instrument: trumpet
Early life: born into poverty, didn't start playing until
he was 12 or 13 when he was put into the Colored
Waifs' Home in New Orleans. Without any formal
musical training, his musical genius was obvious from
the start.

Claim to fame: see above - he was a genius. He invented
the art of improvising a jazz solo, based loosely on a
melody but taking off in all directions. Armstrong
went to Chicago in 1922 to play with King Oliver's
band and from there he never looked back.

Music: Armstrong played the trumpet with a beautiful warm sound. He knew how to pull a melody around, stretching the notes like a rubber band. His *Hot Fives* and *Hot Sevens* recordings changed the face of jazz, and possibly the course of music. Wow!

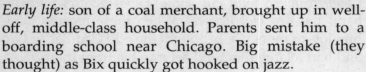

BIX BEIDERBECKE

Born: 10 March 1903, Iowa
Died: 7 August 1931
Instrument: cornet
Early life: son of a coal merchant, brought up in well-off, middle-class household. Parents sent him to a boarding school near Chicago. Big mistake (they thought) as Bix quickly got hooked on jazz.

Claim to fame: first great white jazz musician, much to his parents' disapproval. Sadly, he drank too much - a problem that was to dog him throughout his life.

Music: clear sound and absolute control over his improvisation. He listened to Louis Armstrong and admired him - but went his own musical way.

DUKE ELLINGTON

(EDWARD KENNEDY ELLINGTON)
Born: 29 April 1899, Washington DC
Died: 24 May 1974
Instrument: piano
Early life: born into a black middle-class, well-off family. He was given the nickname 'Duke' when he was a teenager because of his natty dressing. Even as

a child he was very self-confident. His mother was very religious and Duke remained a religious man throughout his life.

Claim to fame: His real instrument was his band. He composed and arranged music for his band, tailoring the music to individual members and the sounds they made.

Music: Duke Ellington didn't just arrange songs - he extended his compositions to create longer, more 'symphonic' jazz forms.

BENNY GOODMAN

Born: 30 May 1909, Chicago
Died: 20 June 1986
Instrument: clarinet
Early life: one of twelve children born to a poor white family. Benny's parents saw music as a good way to escape the poverty-trap, and by 14 he was a professional clarinet player playing in the clubs of Chicago.

Claim to fame: as a bandleader started the craze for Swing and Swing bands.

Music: Goodman's fingers were unbelievably well-trained - he could play anything. He was known for his large swing bands, but he also played in smaller groups in which black and white musicians played together for almost the first time.

BILLIE HOLIDAY

Born: 7 April 1915, Baltimore
Died: 17 July 1959
Instrument: singer
Early life: Later in life wrote a famous autobiography called *Lady Sings the Blues*. According to this Billie had a terrible childhood. Some time around 1930 things started to look up when she sang a song *Body And Soul* to a nightclub audience and reduced them all to tears.

Claim to fame: Billie worked with many of the jazz greats, and soon became a 'great' herself.

Music: a fantastically raw and expressive voice. Billie knew how to sing the blues.

CHARLIE PARKER

Born: August 29, 1920, Kansas City
Died: 12 March 1955
Instrument: alto and tenor saxophone
Early life: son of a doting mother. Musically, he was entirely self-taught which meant he learned how to do some pretty weird but quite useful things.

Claim to fame: started Bebop - whatever everyone else did in music he didn't do. He was a complete rebel in music and in life. Parker died from too much of everything at the early age of 34.

Music: Bebop was a reaction to swing with its irregular beats and odd-length solos.

MILES DAVIS

Born: 25 May 1926, Illinois
Died: 28 September 1991
Instrument: trumpet
Early life: born to well-off parents (his
father was a dentist) who did not want their son to
become a musician. He went to the Juilliard School of
Music in New York to please his parents but soon
became obsessed with jazz - specifically with Charlie
Parker. He even moved in with Parker for a time.

Claim to fame: developed another new style known as
Cool. Listen to *Kind of Blue* made in the late 1950s.

Music: unlike previous soloists who tended to show
off with lots of notes, Davis played short, unconnected
phrases in a lean tone.

JOHN COLTRANE

Born: 23 September 1926, North
Carolina
Died: 17 August 1967
Instrument: Soprano and Tenor
saxophone
Early life: an unremarkable and
comfortable childhood. Coltrane
played in local church and school
bands. He didn't really start his jazz career until he
was in his 20s. Then he played with the Miles Davis
band, swopping solos with Davis himself.

Claim to fame: listen to recordings *Giant Steps* and *My
Favorite Things* for examples of free-style jazz.

Music: Coltrane played 'sheets-of-sound' music - endless pourings out of notes that sometimes held an audience enthralled for a very long time...

ELLA FITZGERALD

Born: 25 April 1920, Virginia
Instrument: singer
Early life: brought up in an orphanage in New York, Ella was 'discovered' at an amateur singing contest when she was 16.

Claim to fame: has appeared and recorded with some of the greatest of jazz greats including Louis Armstrong and Duke Ellington.

Music: developed individual style of 'scat' singing - singing like an instrument without words.

FROM PRESLEY
TO BRITPOP

In fact, things weren't so simple. Many young white people were bored with the sentimental music played on white radio stations. They wanted something faster, tougher - more rebellious. They began to tune into the black music channels and to buy records by black artists. Then along came Bill Haley and the Comets with *Rock Around The Clock*.

Did you know:

? that many black rhythm'n'blues singers had been rocking'n'rolling before Bill Haley came on the scene, but because they were black no one took much notice. It was only when a white singer started playing 'black' music that rock'n'roll really got going...

? that an American DJ called Alan Freed began to play black hits from the rhythm'n'blue charts on a white radio station. Freed also claimed to have invented the term *rock'n'roll*.

? that many white pop singers recorded songs originally written by black rhythm'n'blues musicians. Often these cover versions were big hits, but little or no credit was given to the black writer/singer who usually remained unkown.

? Elvis Presley's first hit *That's All Right Mama* was written by a black singer called Arthur 'Big Boy' Crudup. Arthur sold the rights to his song for a pittance - Elvis went on to make a fortune and Arthur died poor and alone in 1974.

THE BLACKBOARD JUNGLE

Rock Around the Clock was released in 1954 but it didn't become a big hit until it was used in the film *The Blackboard Jungle* in 1955. The film was about a young teacher at a school in New York. The teacher has a tough time with some violent students but he eventually wins their respect. The film was violent and aggressive - and rock'n'roll quickly became associated with rebellion. This was exactly what young people wanted, but their parents weren't so keen... *Blackboard Jungle* had kids jiving in the aisles of the cinemas in the USA and in Britain.

ROCK'N'ROLL RIOTS

ROCK'N'ROLL TERROR

CALL FOR BLACKBOARD JUNGLE BAN

POLICE CALLED TO CINEMA

Bill Haley was followed by Chuck Berry with *Maybelline* and Little Richard with *Tutti Frutti* which contains one of the best lines in the whole of rock'n'roll:

AWOP-BOP-ALOOBOP-ALOP-BAM-BOOM

VILE GYRATIONS

When Elvis Presley appeared as a special guest on a TV show in 1956 he was shown from the waist upwards only. His bottom half was considered to be far too provocative! Elvis's amazing swivelling hips quickly earned him the title of 'Elvis the Pelvis' and the disapproval of grown-ups all over America. Some towns banned his concerts, but nothing could stop Elvis and his fans rockin' and rollin' to hits such as *Heartbreak Hotel*, *All Shook Up* and *Jailhouse Rock*.

Elvis's early hits combined the rhythm and beat of rhythm'n'blues with the melodic style of country music. It confused people. Was this 'black' music or 'white' music? Elvis's fans didn't care - they just loved those dark good looks and sexy style!

There couldn't have been more of a contrast between Elvis the Pelvis and the other great hit of the 1950s, Buddy Holly. Buddy Holly wore a smart suit and tie, and sported a pair of horn-rimmed glasses. No swivelling hips for him on stage - he looked just like the kind of young man your mother would love you to bring home. But Buddy Holly was a seriously talented musician, very influenced by rhythm'n'blues, country, and by Elvis's sound.

Buddy Holly and the Crickets had their first major hit in 1957 with *That'll Be The Day*. They followed this up with *Peggy Sue*. Then tragedy struck. In 1959, Buddy was on tour with three other members of his band. They decided to take a plane to avoid a long and tiring road journey, but there was only room on the plane for three. So they drew lots to decide who should go by road. Buddy and two others got on the plane - but this was to be their last journey. The plane crashed into a field in Iowa and everyone on board was killed. Buddy Holly was only 22 years old.

ODD ONE OUT

Can you spot the odd one out of this list?

THE JERK   THE TWIST   THE PONY
THE LIMBO
THE HOOPLE
THE HAND JIVE   THE MOONWALK
THE POGO   THE STRUT   THE FLY
THE JIVE   THE LOCOMOTION
THE HITCHHIKER
THE POPEYE

THE JITTERBUG

Answer the Hoople is the odd one out. All the rest are names of dances.

ACROSS THE ATLANTIC

Date: the 1960s
Place: Britain
The phenomenon: The Beatles

The Beatles may have started out singing cover versions of 1950s songs, but they quickly developed their own style of music. They wrote and performed their own songs and had their first No.1 hit in 1963 with *Please, Please Me*. The Fab Four (John Lennon, Paul McCartney, George Harrison and Ringo Star) wore neat collarless suits and had pudding-bowl haircuts. They became teen idols and wherever they went they were mobbed by hordes of screaming and hysterical fans. They were big in the USA too. At one point they were nos 1,2,3,4 and 5 in the US charts with five different songs!

The Beatles started the 'Liverpool sound', a completely new direction in pop music. They took inspiration from a very English kind of folk sound, and combined this with a rock beat. The Beatles carried on experimenting with their music right up until the band broke up in 1970. They used mixtures of orchestral and rock instruments, they introduced new instruments such as the sitar into the pop world, and they wrote songs in many, many different styles.

THE REBELLIOUS STONES

If The Beatles were the 'good boys' of pop and rock (even though they rebelled against this image later in their career), the Rolling Stones were the 'bad boys' of the 1960s. The music of the Stones was inspired by black American blues and rhythm'n'blues singers, and they knew how to rock'n'roll. They also knew how to get a reaction with their provocative behaviour on stage, bad language, outrageous dress etc. etc. As usual, kids loved them and adults were outraged. They had their first no 1 hit with *(I Can't Get No) Satisfaction* in 1965.

ALSO IN THE 1960s...

While the Beatles and Stones were wowing audiences on both sides of the Atlantic Ocean, many new kinds of pop and rock were emerging. How many of these have you heard of before?

SURF ROCK:
celebrated the sound and lifestyle of sun-drenched Californian beaches.
Band: the Beach Boys.
Charting singles: *Surfin' USA*; *Good Vibrations*

FOLK ROCK:
started off as a movement in the USA to get back to folk roots. Then Bob Dylan did the unthinkable and added electric guitar sound to a folk song. Many folk rock artists wrote political words to their songs, highlighting what they saw as injustices in society.
Singers/bands: Joan Baez, the Byrds, Bob Dylan, Simon and Garfunkel
Charting singles/albums: *Mr Tambourine Man*; *Blowin' In The Wind*; *Like a Rollin' Stone* (Bob Dylan); *Bridge Over Troubled Water* (Simon and Garfunkel)

ACID ROCK:

or *psychedelic rock*. The 1960s was a time of experiments with mind-altering drugs such as LSD ('acid') which were legal in the USA until 1966. Acid rock went hand-in-hand with the massive protest movement in the USA against war - particularly the Vietnam War.

Bands: Jefferson Airplane, The Doors, The Grateful Dead

Charting singles/albums: *Somebody To Love*; *Light My Fire*; *Live Dead*

SOUL:

music sung and played by black American musicians. Soul was promoted by two independent record labels, Motown in Detroit (from the nickname for Detroit 'motor town') and Stax-Atlantic. The 1960s was the time of the civil rights movement in the USA, the fight for equal rights for black and white. Many songs by soul artists expressed the feelings of black people committed to this struggle...

Bands/singers: Otis Redding, Aretha Franklin, Martha and the Vandellas, Marvin Gaye, James Brown, Smokey Robinson, Diana Ross and the Supremes, The Temptations

Charting singles/albums: *Dancing In The Street* (Martha and the Vandellas); *Respect* (Otis Redding); *I Heard it Through The Grapevine* (Marvin Gaye); *Keep Me Hangin' On* (Supremes)

EVERYTHING GOES BIG

The 1970s was the decade of big. Bands became 'supergroups' who used vast amounts of complicated equipment, went on mega-tours all over the world, made hit albums instead of singles, and made megabucks for themselves and for their record companies. Some of the most super of the supergroups were Jefferson, Lake and Palmer; Crosby, Stills and Nash; Pink Floyd; Fleetwood Mac; the Eagles; Led Zeppelin; Supertramp; Deep Purple; Genesis. Dressing up became big when Alice Cooper and others started looking very 'Glam' on stage. Noise was also big, as the heavy metal bands blew the ears off their audiences with decibel levels equal to those of an aeroplane taking off...

HOW TO BE GLAM

ROLE MODELS: DAVID BOWIE, GARY GLITTER, ALICE COOPER, QUEEN, ROXY MUSIC, MARG BOLAN

PERMED OR SLICKED BACK HAIR

SHINY CLOTHES WITH SEQUINS, SPANGLES AND GLITTER

GLAMMED UP GUITAR

PLATFORM BOOTS

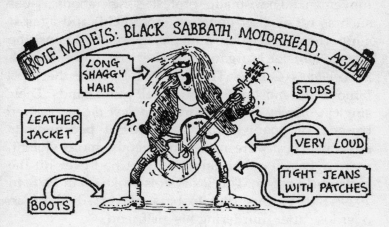

By the middle of the '70s, a lot of rock musicians were very, very rich. They could live where they wanted to live and they could make the music they wanted to make. They had no reason any more to be rebellious against the older generation... they were the older generation!! As usual in the history of rock and pop, as soon as things settled down there was a reaction. In fact it was a revolution. It started in Britain in 1976, and it was PUNK.

CHAOS AND DISORDER

'The basic idea in punk is to turn children against their parents.' - Johnny Rotten: The Sex Pistols

Anyone could be a punk. You didn't have to be rich or famous, you didn't have to be talented, you didn't even have to be able to play an instrument or sing. Have your hair cut into spikes or a Mohican, wear a few safety pins and chains, army surplus gear, dark glasses - you are a punk. Now sneer.

The Clash were the most musical band of the punk movement. They made protest songs about issues such as racial discrimination (apartheid) and against supporters of racist movements, as well as against the Prime Minister Margaret Thatcher and had hits such as *London's Calling*. The Sex Pistols were the most famous and most outrageous of all punk bands. Their singles *Anarchy in the UK* and *God Save the Queen* were banned by many radio stations but became hits anyway. They were more outrageous, more violent, more aggressive than anything that had ever hit the rock world before. The Sex Pistols broke up in 1978. In 1979, Sid Vicious (the ex-bass player) died of an overdose after murdering his girlfriend.

ROMANTIC REACTIONS

And out of punk came... the New Romantics and New Wave.

How to recognise a New Romantic:
Not difficult. Look for distinguishing features such as frilly shirts, swashbuckling pirate/highwayman outfits, feathers and velvet ribbons, suede boots, lace and bows.

AND FINALLY

After the 80s? The 90s of course! House and rave, Britpop and boy bands (and girl bands), trip-hop and Indie music - what will we think of as '90s music' in years to come? Well, that's partly up to you ...

STUDIO TALK

You've fixed your band, you've written your first hit, you've booked a studio. Now all you have to do is understand the language of studios. Can you pick out the correct meanings to these studio jargon words?

1. foldback

a) the amount of turn-up on your jeans. b) monitors or headphones that allow you to hear what you are playing. c) a repeated passage in the music.

2. click track

a) a steady series of clicks heard through headphones to allow players to keep in time. b) groovy clicking fingers. c) unwanted noise and clicks heard on the finished recording.

3. DAT

a) a kind of fly-swatter. b) stands for Digital Audio Tape. c) the opposite of DIS.

4. rumble

a) what your stomach does after six hours of recording. b) the noise of the Underground trains beneath the recording studio. c) any unwanted low-level noise on the final recording.

5. anechoic chamber

a) a room with no echo. b) a room with a serious illness. c) an underwater room.

Answers: 1b; 2a; 3b; 4c; 5a.

TOP TEN OF POP AND ROCK

ELVIS PRESLEY

Born: 8 January 1935
Died: 16 August 1977
Full name: Elvis Aaron Presley
Greatest hits: *Heartbreak Hotel, Blue Suede Shoes, Jailhouse Rock, Love Me Tender, It's Now Or Never*
High point: the original rocking'n'-rolling, hip swivellin', 1950s rebel.
Low point: towards the end of his life the 'King' was overweight, ill from drug abuse and completely worn out. He died from heart failure.

THE BEATLES

Paul McCartney (18 June 1942)
John Lennon (9 October 1940 - 8 December 1980)
George Harrison (25 February 1943)
Ringo Starr (7 July 1940)
Greatest hits: *Please, Please Me, I Want To Hold Your Hand, A Hard Day's Night, Help, Yesterday, Sergeant Pepper's Lonely Heart's Club Band, Hey Jude, Let It Be, Get Back*
High point: 26 November 1962. The Beatles record the whole of their first album *Please, Please Me* in one day. The album went to No. 1 in the charts in May 1963 and was the beginning of the Beatles' huge influence on

the course of rock and pop music.

Low point: the split-up of the group in 1970, accompanied by lawsuits and bitterness.

ROLLING STONES

Original line-up:

Mick Jagger (26 July 1943)

Keith Richards (18 December 1943)

Brian Jones (28 February 1942 - 3 July 1969)

Bill Wyman (23 October 1936)

Charlie Watts (2 June 1941)

Greatest hits: *Satisfaction*, *Jumping Jack Flash*, *Paint It Black*, *Lady Jane*, *Let's Spend The Night Together*, *Honky Tonk Woman*, *Miss You*, and albums *Beggar's Banquet* and *Some Girls*

High point: they are the longest-lasting rock band ever.

Low point: Brian Jones drowned shortly after leaving the band.

BOB DYLAN

Born: 24 May 1941

Real name: Robert Allen Zimmerman

Greatest hits: *Blowin' In The Wind* (performed by Peter, Paul and Mary), *The Times They Are A'Changin*, *Mr Tambourine Man* (performed by the Byrds), *Like A Rolling Stone*, *Lay Lady Lay*

High point: booed by the audience at Newport Folk Festival in 1965 for playing an electric guitar, BUT Dylan was in the business of knocking down musical barriers and this was a big one.

Low point: Motorbike crash in July 1966 which led to semi-retirement for over a year.

JIMI HENDRIX

Born: 27 November 1942
Died: 18 September 1970
Full name: Johnny
Allen Hendrix
Greatest hits: *Hey Joe, Purple Haze, The Wind Cries Mary,* and albums *Are You Experienced, Axis: Bold As Love, Electric Ladyland*
High points: with the backing of his band the Jimi Hendrix Experience, Jimi was continually experimenting and pushing the potential of the guitar further and further. He reached parts of the guitar no one had ever explored before!
Low point: Hendrix became exhausted by the demands and the lifestyle of stardom. He died after taking too many sleeping tablets at the early age of 27.

DAVID BOWIE

Born: 8 April 1947
Real name: David
Robert Jones
Greatest hits: *Space Oddity, The Rise And Fall Of Ziggy Stardust & The Spiders From Mars, Young Americans, Fame, Ashes To Ashes, Let's Dance, Dancing in the Street* (with Mick Jagger)
High point: Bowie as Ziggy Stardust.
Low point: Bowie's appearance in the disastrous film musical *Absolute Beginners*.

ELTON JOHN

Born: 25 March 1947

Real name: Reginald Kenneth Dwight

Greatest hits: *Your Song, Rocket Man, Crocodile Rock, Bennie & The Jets, Don't Go Breaking My Heart* (with Kiki Dee) *Healing Hands/Sacrifice, Candle in the Wind* and albums *Don't Shoot Me I'm Only The Piano Player, Goodbye Yellow Brick Road*

High points: musically the double album *Goodbye Yellow Brick Road*. Personally it could be the moment that Elton John became chairman of Watford Football Club which he has supported since his youth.

Low point: Elton John was just the sort of rich, glam rock star that punk was directed against.

BOB MARLEY

Born: 6 February 1945

Died: 11 May 1981

Greatest hits: *Get Up Stand Up, I Shot The Sherriff, No Woman No Cry, Jammin', Exodus, Could You Be Loved* and albums *Babylon By Bus, Burning*

High points: with his Rastafarian faith and strong political views, Bob Marley worked throughout his life for world peace and understanding. Bob Marley and his backing group, the Wailers, also pioneered a new sound in music - reggae.

Low points: In 1976, Marley, his wife and manager were shot by would-be assassins in Jamaica. They all survived. Sadly, Bob Marley did not survive a cancer which killed him in 1981.

MADONNA

Born: 16 August 1958
Full name: Madonna Louise Ciccone
Greatest hits: *Like a Virgin*, *Into the Groove*, *Holiday*, *Crazy For You*
High point: the phenomenally successful *Blonde Ambition* world tour of 1990.
Low point: Madonna's early life was hard. Her mother died when she was young, leaving six children. Madonna spent much of her time minding the family before being sent to a convent school.

MICHAEL JACKSON

Born: 29 August 1958
Full name: Michael Joseph Jackson
Greatest hits: *Don't Stop*, *Rock With You*, *Off The Wall*, *She's Out Of My Life*, *Billie Jean*, *Beat It*, *Thriller*, and albums *Thriller*, *Bad*
High points: was a child star with his brothers in the *Jackson Five*. Went on to become a megastar and to make some of the most innovative videos to promote the singles of his album *Thriller*.
Low points: rumours abound about nose jobs, face lifts, skin whiteners - all denied.

118

QUIZ

You've read the book, now try answering these musical posers...

1. Gregorian chant was named after:
a) Pope Gregory I
b) Pope Gregory II
c) Nobody's sure

2. Guido's Hand was a useful device for:
a) Helping with the dishes
b) Memorising music
c) Playing the lute

3. *Cori spezzati* means
a) Spaced choirs
b) 'Spaced-out' choirs
c) It's a new type of pizza from the local takeaway

4. Frederick the Great loved opera. If his opera singers didn't do exactly as he told them he:
a) Talked to them nicely
b) Put them in prison
c) Bought them an ice-cream

5. Johann Ambrosius Bach was J.S. Bach's:
a) Father
b) First cousin
c) First cousin twice removed

6. One of the biggest traffic jams of all time was caused by:
a) Handel's carriage which got stuck in the mud
b) Handel's *Water Music*
c) Handel's *Fireworks Music*

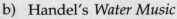

7. A string quartet has:
a) A violin, a viola, a cello, a double bass
b) Two violins, a viola, a cello
c) Two violins, a cello, a double bass

8. Theobald Boehm was responsible for updating the:
a) Clarinet
b) Tuba
c) Flute

9. Which of Beethoven's nine symphonies is known as the *Eroica*?
a) No. 2
b) No. 3
c) No. 7

10. Hector Berlioz was madly in love with:
a) Harriet Smithson
b) Harriet Smith
c) Henrietta Smithy

11. Musical parties held to hear Schubert's latest music were called:
a) Schubertfests
b) Schubertiads
c) Schubert's Musical Parties

12. Which composer liked to collect birdsong?
a) Bela Bartók
b) Olivier Messiaen
c) Claude Debussy

13. What's odd about John Cage's piece 4'33"?
a) It's silent throughout
b) It's for prepared piano
c) It uses pre-recorded tapes

14. Which city is thought of as the home of jazz - where it all started?
a) Chicago
b) Milton Keynes
c) New Orleans

15. What instrument did Miles Davis play?
a) Cornet
b) Saxophone
c) Trumpet

16. Who wrote Elvis Presley's first hit *That's All Right Mama?*
a) Elvis Presley
b) Arthur 'Big Boy' Crudup
c) Bill Haley

17. What is surf rock?
a) A type of music celebrating the Californian lifestyle
b) What you have to avoid when you're surfing
c) A type of rock music with an uneven beat

18. Where was the Motown label originally based?
a) New York
b) Chicago
c) Detroit

19. Which of these wasn't Glam?
a) David Bowie
b) Motorhead
c) Roxy Music

20. Who wrote the hit song *I shot the sheriff*?
a) Eric Clapton
b) Michael Jackson
c) Bob Marley

Answers 1c; 2b; 3a; 4b; 5a; 6c; 7b; 8c; 9b; 10a; 11b; 12b; 13a; 14c; 15c; 16b; 17a; 18c; 19b; 20c

INDEX

jazz 54, 93-102
John, Elton 117
Josquin des Prez 22

Lieder 67-70
Liszt, Franz 56
Lully, Jean-Baptiste 32-3

Machaut, Guillaume de 19
Madonna 118
Marley, Bob 117
Mendelssohn, Fanny 80-1
Mendelssohn, Felix 81
Messiaen, Olivier 83, 87, 90
monody 27
Monteverdi, Claudio 28-31, 73, 80
Morton, Jelly Roll 97
motet 37, 40
Mozart, Wolfgang Amadeus 8, 46, 47- 51, 57, 59, 93

New Romantics 112

Ondes martenot 90
opera 26-35, 41, 42, 44, 47, 48, 51, 60, 68, 73-7, 80, 95
oratorio 35, 41, 42, 44

Paganini, Nicolo 55, 56
Palestrina, Giovanni Perluigi da 23
Parker, Charlie 96, 100, 101
Passion 35, 37, 39, 41
Peri, Jacopo 27, 28, 29
piano 48, 54, 56, 59, 60, 67, 68, 69, 70, 71-2, 82, 83, 88, 89, 97, 98
plainchant 10-15

polyphony 15, 18-25, 26
Presley, Elvis 104, 105, 106, 114
printing 20-1
Puccini, Giacomo 76, 77
punk 111-2, 117

Ragtime 94-5
recitative 35
recorder 52, 58, 89
reggae 117
Rolling Stones 107-8, 115
Rossini, Gioacchino 73

Saxophone 54, 100, 101
Schubert, Franz Peter 67-8, 70, 93
Schumann, Clara 68-9, 71-2
Schumann, Robert 67, 68-9, 71-2
Segovia, Andres 56-7
Smyth, Ethel 82-3
soul 109
Stockhausen, Karlheinz 91
Stradivari, Antonio 57
Strauss, Richard 76
Stravinsky, Igor 84-5
string quartet 47, 48, 51, 60, 67
Strozzi, Barbara 80
surf rock 108
symphonies 44, 48, 49, 51, 60, 61-4, 66, 68, 69, 83, 84, 95

Tallis, Thomas 22-3, 24
Tchaikovsky, Pyotr 74, 75
theremin 54, 90
troubadours 17, 18

NOW READ ON

If you want to know more about the story of music, see if your local library or bookshop has any of these books.

A YOUNG PERSON'S GUIDE TO MUSIC
by Neil Ardley (Dorling Kindersley) (includes CD)

INTRODUCING BACH
by Roland Vernon (Belitha Press)

INTRODUCTING BEETHOVEN
by Roland Vernon (Belitha Press)

THE WORLD OF MUSIC
by Nicola Barber and Mary Mure (Evans Brothers)(includes CD)

OXFORD CHILDREN'S A-Z OF MUSIC
by Humphrey Carpenter, Paul Keene, Christine Ward (Oxford University Press)

THE KINGFISHER BOOK OF MUSIC
(Kingfisher Books)

ACKNOWLEDGEMENTS

The author and publishers are grateful for permission to reproduce the following extracts quoted in this book:

Extract from Mozart's letter page 50, taken from *The Letters of Mozart & His Family* edited by Emily Anderson, published by Macmillan Press Ltd.

Extract under the title "A somewhat savage aspect" pages 60-61, taken from Schindler, *Beethoven 1845* quoted in *World of Art: Beethoven* Robbins Landon 1970, published by Thames & Hudson Ltd.

The Ghostly Double (Schubert) page 70, based on a translation in *The Schubert Song Companion* by John Reed, translations by Norma Deane and Celia Larner, 1985, published by Manchester University Press.

Trouvères' song page 79, taken from *Women and Music: a history* by Karen Pendele 1991, published by Indiana University Press.

Poem page 84, from the Boston *Herald* (1924), taken from *Words About Music* by John Amis and Michael Rose (1989), published by Faber and Faber Ltd.

OTHER BOOKS IN THIS SERIES